W9-BAF-593

Steve Parish
PUBLISHING

A Wild Australia Guide

MAMMALS

STEVE PARISH & KARIN COX

Contents

Introduction

Class Mammalia is one of the most diverse classes in the animal kingdom. Mammals vary in size from the diminutive Bumblebee Bat of South-East Asia (at just 30 mm long) to the enormous, 30 m long Blue Whale — the largest animal ever known to have lived. Australia, with its long period of isolation from other continents, has gradually evolved a unique mammalian fauna. This continent is blessed with 356 living native mammal species and 23 introduced species — 24 if you count humans, since we are also mammals. Unfortunately, this number excludes the 27 mammals that have succumbed to extinction since human occupation of the continent. Included in the class Mammalia are the sea mammals known as cetaceans, such as dolphins, Dugongs and whales. These sea mammals are dealt with in another Wild Australia Guide and are not featured prominently in this book.

Some of the continent's surviving terrestrial mammals, such as the Koala and the Red Kangaroo, have become synonymous with this land and are recognisable icons of the country. Others, such as the tiny Cape York Melomys, are little-known and even more rarely seen. Despite having many differences in size, profile, habitat and behaviour, all mammals share a number of common traits — all are vertebrates that are covered in body hair (even when "naked" some hair remains), all suckle their young on milk produced by the mother's body, and all have lower jaws that attach straight onto their skulls. Mammals' teeth are also distinctive — they vary in shape and size, and scientists often use them to differentiate one species from another.

Above: Koalas are unique, highly specialised arboreal mammals. **Right:** Nocturnal Sugar Gliders belong to the family of wrist-winged gliders. **Opposite:** Kangaroos and other macropods are familiar herbivorous mammals.

A History of Mammals

Mammals began appearing in the fossil record in rocks dating back to the Mesozoic Era around 220 million years ago. By the end of the era, all of the major mammalian groups were in existence. It is thought that they may have evolved from the dinosaurs when Australia was still part of the supercontinent known as Gondwana. Fossil evidence suggests that monotremes were the first group to diverge, showing distinct differences from other mammals by 150 million years ago. Placental and marsupial mammals appear to have split from each other at some point before 100 million years ago. So far, the earliest marsupial fossil found in Australia dates from 55 million years ago.

Today, Australia is unique in being the only place on the planet where the three different types of mammals — placentals, marsupials and monotremes — are all found. With the exception of South America, most other countries contain only placental mammals.

Below: The first fossil mammal found in Australia was *Diprotodon optatum*, which was similar to today's wombats. It weighed 2 tonnes and is the largest Australian mammal ever found.

Most Australian flora and fauna can trace their lineage back to the giant southern landmass of Gondwana. When Australia was cast adrift from Antarctica about 45 million years ago, continental drift carried the country northwards and its climate, landforms, vegetation and fauna underwent a series of gradual changes. Climate alternated from ice ages to warm spells, and sea levels consequently rose and fell. Natural selection favoured those mammals that were able to adapt and exploit new environments. During the Eocene Epoch (53–34 million years ago), marsupials began to dominate the terrestrial fauna of Australia. Also in the Eocene Epoch, placental mammals made their first appearance, with bats flying to these shores around 55 million years ago. In the wet rainforests of the Miocene Epoch (23–5.3 million years ago), marsupials reached their highest levels of diversity. Sea mammals are relative newcomers to Australia, having arrived 28–23 million years ago.

Over the past 5 million years, the continent has been drying out. Woodlands and grasslands have gradually become Australia's dominant vegetation. In the increasingly arid conditions, animals that were efficient users of energy and water, and that could breed rapidly following infrequent rains, began to flourish. Consequently, around 4 million years ago, rodents were on the rise. Other remarkable beasts were also at large (quite literally!) during this time. Known as megafauna, these gigantic mammals were related to today's wombats, kangaroos and echidnas, which evolved around 5 million years ago. From 68,000 years ago, sudden mass extinctions occurred and by 35,000 years ago megafauna had vanished. It is thought that the loss of sheltering habitat due to fire, coupled with human hunting, hastened their demise. From 1788, European settlement has introduced newer mammal species, many of which have been detrimental and compete with Australia's native mammals.

MEGAFAUNA

During the Pleistocene Epoch, megafauna roamed the continent. These giant mammals included *Procoptodon goliath*, a 2.5 m high kangaroo; *Propleopus*, a flesh-eating kangaroo (below, on display at Riversleigh Fossil Centre) and the carnivorous marsupial lion, *Thylacoleo carnifex*, which weighed about 150 kg. All megafauna became extinct 68–35,000 years ago. Why this happened is unclear, but it is thought climate change, hunting by humans, or disease may have been responsible.

Australian Mammal Groups

There are three main groups of mammals — all of which are found in Australia and all of which reproduce differently. While all suckle their young on milk produced by the mother's mammary glands, not all mammals give birth to live young. Australia and New Guinea are the only places in the world where egg-laying monotreme mammals exist. Marsupials give birth to live young, but the young are "premature" and require further development in a pouch. The offspring of placental mammals develop inside the mother's body, nourished by the placenta, which connects a baby to its mother's blood vessels and body.

MONOTREMES

Monotreme translates as "one hole" — in reference to the cloaca, which is a single opening for reproductive and waste purposes. Australia has two monotreme species; both are egg-layers. Young monotremes are nourished by yolk inside soft-shelled eggs, which the mother incubates. Echidnas incubate their eggs in a pouch, but Platypuses brood their eggs inside a nesting burrow dug into a creek bed. When the egg hatches, the young monotreme is naked, blind and underdeveloped. Female monotremes produce milk from their mammary glands, but have no nipples; instead, the milk dribbles onto a patch on the stomach and is suckled by the young.

MARSUPIALS

Marsupials give birth to underdeveloped young that must be nourished in the mother's pouch after birth. After a short gestation period, baby marsupials are born furless, blind and with poorly formed hindlimbs. Using their forelimbs, they struggle from their mother's cloaca, through her fur, to a teat on a fold or flap of skin (known as a pouch, or marsupium) on the abdomen. It is here that the offspring continues its development. Some pouches open at the top, while others, such as the wombat's, open at the bottom so that debris does not enter the pouch when the wombat is digging. Not all marsupials have a fully developed pouch, although most do.

PLACENTALS

Embryos of most mammals develop inside the mother's uterus. In placental mammals, the embryo can be nourished in the uterus because it is attached to the mother's body through the placenta, which connects the mother's blood vessels to the baby. At birth, the baby is expelled from the uterus. Unlike other mammal groups, placentals have an anus for defecation and a separate opening for reproduction and urination. Some placental young, such as mice, are born blind and naked; others are small, fully formed versions of their parents. All placental babies suckle until they can feed themselves.

AUSTRALIAN MAMMAL GROUPS

MONOTREMES	MARSUPIALS	PLACENTALS
Platypus	Quolls, dunnarts and relatives	Bats
Echidna	Thylacine and Tasmanian Devil	Rodents
	Numbat	Dingo
	Marsupial moles	Seals and sea-lions
	Bilby and bandicoots	Whales and dolphins
	Koala and wombats	Dugong
	Possums and gliders	
	Kangaroos, wallabies and relatives	

Where Do Mammals Live?

Australia's terrestrial mammals occupy a diverse number of environments. Australia's mammals have evolved in conjunction with particular habitats and native vegetation, and many enjoy co-dependent and mutually beneficial relationships with endemic flora. Natural regimes of fire, flood and seasons, particularly in Australia's north, are crucial to the survival of some species. Other species are hardy and arid-adapted and can even exist on seawater! Many species use a variety of habitats, moving from one "sheltering" environment to their preferred feeding grounds. Forest fringes and habitat "edges", where different types of vegetation overlap, are especially important for many mammal species.

ARIDLANDS

Most of the mammals that live in deserts or in Australia's desiccated inland are nocturnal and conserve energy by resting under shade or in burrows during the day. The most common desert-dwellers are native mice and small marsupials such as some of the bettongs. Red Kangaroos are also able to live in dry regions.

FORESTS AND RAINFORESTS

Tree-kangaroos, possums, gliders and some bat species are primarily rainforest-dwellers. Forests and rainforests provide shelter by way of foliage and tree hollows, as well as food such as forest fruit, lichen, mosses and invertebrates in the leaf litter. Grassy clearings close to forests attract forest-living grazers such as pademelons.

OPEN WOODLANDS AND COASTAL HEATH

Open woodlands in Australia's hinterland often abut agricultural land or grassy cleared areas, which are prime feeding grounds for macropods. Some small marsupial species (particularly nectarivores) live close to the coast, sheltering in the flowering plants of coastal heath, such as banksia and grevillea. Some bats also roost in paperbark trees near the coast.

Left: Grasslands provide sustenance for many macropod species.

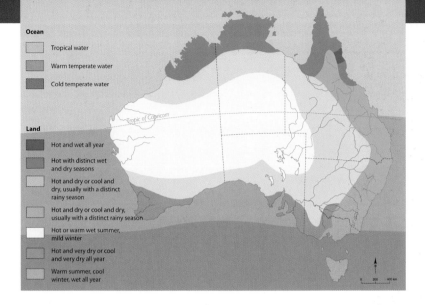

Ocean

- Tropical water
- Warm temperate water
- Cold temperate water

Land

- Hot and wet all year
- Hot with distinct wet and dry seasons
- Hot and dry or cool and dry, usually with a distinct rainy season
- Hot and dry or cool and dry, usually with a distinct rainy season
- Hot or warm wet summer, mild winter
- Hot and very dry or cool and very dry all year
- Warm summer, cool winter, wet all year

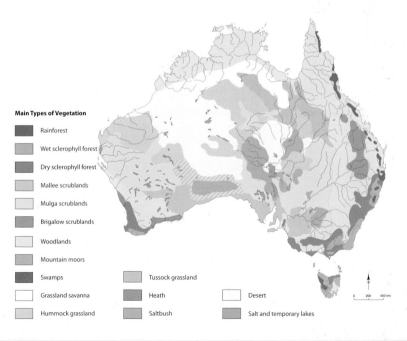

Main Types of Vegetation

- Rainforest
- Wet sclerophyll forest
- Dry sclerophyll forest
- Mallee scrublands
- Mulga scrublands
- Brigalow scrublands
- Woodlands
- Mountain moors
- Swamps
- Grassland savanna
- Hummock grassland
- Tussock grassland
- Heath
- Saltbush
- Desert
- Salt and temporary lakes

Floodplains

Sandy deserts

Stony deserts

Temperate forests

Grasslands

Heathlands

Mulga woodlands

Tropical rainforests

Alpine grasslands

Caves

Stony plateaus

Tropical woodlands

Protecting Native Mammals

In Australia, as in other countries, humans must learn to coexist comfortably with native animals and help protect their environments. Most Australians come into contact with native mammals many times over their lives. They see mammals in national parks and reserves, encounter them near campsites or backyards, or view them at zoos and wildlife parks. Some people even end up as "adoptive parents" to orphaned mammal babies. Many species are conspicuous and regularly seen, even in suburban and urban areas. Possums are renowned for residing in the roofs and ceilings of buildings, and kangaroos and wallabies are frequent visitors to farmlands, golf courses and campgrounds — almost anywhere with plenty of fresh, green grass. Other species are shy and difficult to find, even for the most experienced nature photographer.

Despite Australia's affinity with mammals, with which we share our taxonomic class, this continent has the most appalling record of mammal extinctions. In just over 200 years of European occupation, 27 mammal species have vanished. For many people, the first sighting they have of a bandicoot is after they have struck it on the road. Similarly, many thousands of native mice and rats fall victim to the human aversion to rodents. Our exploding population, and subsequent land clearing and deforestation for agriculture and property development, has also had a devastating impact on mammals, fleeing them of natural habitats they have become superbly adapted to over millions of years. Another human contribution to the decline in native mammals is the introduction of domestic mammals, either as stock or, in the case of the Red Fox and the rabbit, for game. The hard hoofs of domestic stock and the practice of overgrazing have added to the problems of erosion and desalination, further destroying the habitats of native species.

It is true that some species have benefited from the increase in crop foods and ground water, such as dams and water troughs, but others have declined

Above, left to right: Sugar Gliders are sociable possums that frequent flowering plants in many backyards; A Northern Brown Bandicoot snacks on the leavings of campers.

Above, left to right: Platypuses in the wild are vulnerable to pollution of waterways. This one is being cared for at Healesville Sanctuary, Victoria; Orphaned bats are fed a special milk formula.

drastically. Even those that have increased in number do not always directly benefit. Kangaroos can reach plague proportions where water and food are plentiful, which has led to licensed culling to keep numbers in check.

The end result is that it is our human responsibility to not only appreciate and learn more about our native mammals, but to try to reverse the effects of human impact on this continent. Today, all native mammals are protected, with the exception of macropod species that are able to be hunted to a strict annual quota. However, roadkill and land clearing still claim many lives each year and often leave young, underdeveloped offspring in need of care. Care organisations, wildlife sanctuaries and dedicated individuals spend many thousands of hours each year making sure injured or orphaned mammals are given a fighting chance at life.

Caring for native wildlife requires a licence and an understanding of how to meet the needs of a particular species. Effective care means providing the animal with a lifestyle that is as close as possible to the quality of life it would experience in the wild. Infant mammals require a special milk formula (as many are lactose intolerant), regular and often inconvenient feed times (as do human babies), and specialist attention, such as stimulation to go to the toilet. Marsupials also need a pouch-like environment to keep them warm. All injured or abandoned wildlife should be examined by a vet before going into care.

Monotremes

Australia is home to the world's only two types of living monotremes — the Platypus and the echidna. Only one species of Platypus exists and is endemic to Australia. There are four echidna species — the Short-beaked Echidna is the only species found in Australia. Three long-beaked echidna species exist in New Guinea.

Both the Platypus and the echidna are egg-laying mammals that belong to the order Monotremata. Both have sensitive, modified "noses" and both have exploited ecological niches that provide them with little competition from other mammals. The similarities, however, end there. They live vastly different lifestyles and have widely discrepant body forms. In fact, so improbable is the Platypus's morphology that when the first specimen was sent to England in the late 1700s it was described as an "amphibious mole" and believed to be an elaborate hoax!

The Platypus spends up to twelve hours a day in the water and is superbly equipped for its semi-aquatic lifestyle, with large, webbed feet and a sensitive bill that is able to detect the weak electrical impulses generated by moving animals. While underwater, its eyes, ears and nostrils are closed, so sweeping the long, flat bill from side to side assists it in detecting its prey. Once prey is caught, it is stored in a cheek pouch and taken to the surface, where it is ground up between horny plates on the Platypus's upper and lower jaws.

Short-beaked Echidnas are one of the few species to be found in almost all of Australia's varied habitats. They are covered with stiff, hollow spines (which are actually modified hairs) that help defend against predators. Echidnas survive on a diet of ants and termites and have squat, short limbs equipped with long, powerful claws for digging into termite mounds. If alarmed, they roll into a ball or quickly dig into the ground.

Above: Echidnas feed exclusively on ants and termites. They track these insects by scent — probing mounds with a long, sensitive snout and tongue. **Opposite:** The Platypus feeds on invertebrates, small fishes and frogs, which it detects underwater with its bill.

Platypus *Ornithorhynchus anatinus*

The Platypus is the sole living member of the family Ornithorhynchidae, although fossil links indicate that several other Platypus-like creatures, such as Steropodon, existed as far back as the Early Cretaceous Period around 150 million years ago. Its unique, somewhat bizarre body combines features that make it superbly adapted for a semi-aquatic lifestyle.

FEATURES: The Platypus is unmistakable, having a duck-like bill, webbed feet and a sleek, brown body that looks somewhat otter-like. The Platypus's thick, insulating fur is made up of a fine inner layer and a water-repellent, oily outer layer that moults continually. Large, webbed front feet allow the Platypus to propel itself through the water. The back feet are also webbed and are used for steering and braking. The broad, paddle-like tail is a fat reserve that also acts as a rudder. Males have a venomous spur on the inner side of each hindfoot.

DIET & HABITAT: Freshwater creeks, rivers and dams in eastern Australia (from north Qld to SA) are their preferred waterways. The bill contains thousands of small "sensors" that detect invertebrates, fishes and frogs.

BEHAVIOUR: Solitary and mostly nocturnal, Platypuses are best seen at dawn and dusk when they are foraging. Much time is spent grooming. When they are not grooming or feeding, they usually rest in a "camping burrow".

BREEDING: Most Platypuses breed from July–Nov after courting for several days. Females lay one to three sticky, 17 mm eggs in a nesting burrow and brood for 10–12 days.

THREATS: Pollution of waterways, foxes, dogs, feral cats and goannas.

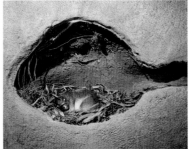

Top: Once they hatch, young platypuses remain in the burrow until they are fully furred at around six weeks. **Above:** Platypuses usually stay submerged for less than a minute. **Opposite, clockwise from top:** On land, Platypuses fold back the webbing and walk on their knuckles; The male's venomous spur; A battle-scarred Platypus dives for food.

DIET: Crayfish and other freshwater invertebrates, small fishes and frogs

LENGTH: HBT 55–63 cm
WEIGHT: 0.7–3.0 kg
STATUS: Endangered (SA); Secure elsewhere

Short-beaked Echidna *Tachyglossus aculeatus*

Echidnas have excellent defence mechanisms. They are covered in hard, hollow spines that jut from the body fur and are shed just once a year. Echidnas are also skilled excavators that can rapidly burrow into the earth if threatened. On hard surfaces they usually freeze, hunching the shoulders so the spines are erect, or they may roll up into a spiky ball. These defensive tactics afford them relative longevity and they may live for up to 50 years.

FEATURES: Colour varies depending on the distribution, but the fur is usually light to dark brown close to the body, with paler protruding spines. The face is furred and spineless with small eyes and a protracted, tubular snout. The tongue, when extended, is almost twice as long as the snout. All five toes on the front feet are clawed; on the back feet, only the second and third toes have claws. Females have a temporary pouch and males have ankle spurs.

DIET & HABITAT: Short-beaked Echidnas show little preference for habitat, provided there are plenty of ants and termites (their sole food source). They occupy habitats across the entire continent from woodlands and aridlands to tropical rainforests.

BEHAVIOUR: Echidnas are nomadic wanderers that forage in a home range of 20–200 ha and shelter under leaves, bushes or in hollow logs on their rambles. They are solitary, and active by day or night in warmer weather.

BREEDING: Depending on the climate, echidnas mate from July–Aug. Many males may pursue the same female. Females develop a temporary flap-like pouch and incubate a single, soft-shelled egg for ten days. When hatched, the "puggle" (as baby echidnas are known) is hairless, developing spines at around three months.

THREATS: Few threats, but often become roadkill. Habitat destruction and pesticides may limit their diet.

Top and above: A baby Echidna or "puggle".
Opposite, clockwise from top: Echidnas move slowly with a waddle-like walk; Echidnas are strong swimmers; Forming a defensive "ball".

DIET: Exclusively ants and termites

LENGTH: HB 30–45 cm
WEIGHT: 2–7 kg
STATUS: Secure and common

Marsupials

The majority of Australia's large native mammals belong to the subclass Marsupialia. Apart from introduced, domestic mammals, marsupials are some of the most highly visible and commonly seen mammals, particularly those in the order Diprotodontia, which includes possums and kangaroos. Others, such as the dasyurids, are less often seen, but include such high-profile species as the Tasmanian Devil.

The first marsupials were recorded in South America, centuries before Australia was discovered. Scientists who discovered them believed the pouch to be an external womb. Of course, we now know that the pouch is more like an infant storage facility that allows the juvenile joey to stay warm and protected while it continues to suckle and develop. Although they are commonly regarded as "pouched mammals", not all marsupials have a pouch — some have just a small, modified flap of skin that swells temporarily to accommodate offspring. Others, such as the Numbat, have no pouch at all. Hence this order is truly defined not by the pouch, but by the common reproductive trait of giving birth to young that is in a very immature state and is later nurtured on its mother's milk to develop outside of the uterus. This gives some marsupials, such as the Red Kangaroo, reproductive benefits, including the ability to have a suspended embryo in the uterus and offspring in the pouch simultaneously. Also remarkable is that some marsupials have opposable "thumbs" — a trait they share only with primates.

Above: Marsupials have a range of body forms.
Sugar Gliders are agile, tree-dwelling marsupials.
Opposite: Koalas are the only tailless marsupials.

Carnivorous Marsupials

Australia has approximately 56 small mammals that belong to the order Dasyuromorphia, which translates as "hairy tail shape". Tails aside, they are differentiated from other marsupials by having three pairs of lower incising teeth, and hindlimbs on which the second and third toes are not fused together.

The majority of animals in this order are small, carnivorous mammals in the family Dasyuridae. Of these, the best known and largest is the Tasmanian Devil. The smallest is the Narrow-nosed Planigale, which may weigh as little as 5 g.

With the exception of the larger Tasmanian Devil and four quoll species, most small dasyurids superficially resemble rodents; however, their faces are generally more pointed and their jaws are full of razor-sharp teeth, rather than the square, chisel-like teeth of rodents. Although small, dasyurids are famously ferocious. They are not fussy eaters and will attack mammals, birds and invertebrates, and even consume carrion. Some, such as *Antechinus* species, are just as assertive when it comes to reproduction. During the breeding season, males expend huge amounts of energy searching for females, mating, and fighting competing males, which results in their death.

The Numbat also belongs to this order, but requires special treatment — it is a one-of-a-kind carnivorous mammal that is the sole member of the family Myrmecobiidae. Existing on a specialised diet of termites, the Numbat's numerous teeth are modified to peg-like structures. Surprisingly, although the Numbat has 25 pairs of teeth — more than any other native terrestrial mammal — most of them are below the gum line and are of little use (given that the Numbat exists solely on termites).

The Tasmanian Devil may be the largest living marsupial carnivore, but this was not always the case. The final and most unfortunate member of the Dasyuromorphia is the now-extinct Thylacine, or Tasmanian Tiger, which belonged to the family Thylacinidae. The last Thylacine died in Hobart Zoo in 1936.

Above: Insects are a common source of prey. **Below:** Nectar, pollen and insects are extracted from nectar-producing plants.

Kultarr *Antechinomys laniger*

In 1856, John Gould drew this small, long-legged marsupial perched on a tree branch; however, it is entirely terrestrial and perfectly adapted to life in open, arid country.

DIET: Mainly insects and spiders

LENGTH: HB 7–10 cm; T 10–15 cm

WEIGHT: 20–30 g

STATUS: Rare (Qld); Endangered (NSW); Near Threatened (NT)

BEHAVIOUR: Kultarrs are solitary and nocturnal, sheltering by day beneath spinifex tussocks, saltbush, in hollow logs and stumps or in abandoned burrows. Despite their long legs, they do not hop but are quadrupedal.

THREATS: Feral cats, foxes, Dingoes and birds of prey.

Fawn Antechinus *Antechinus bellus*

This is the palest and one of the largest Antechinus *species. It was once considered very rare but is now quite common within its isolated range.*

DIET: Almost entirely insects

LENGTH: HB 11–14.8 cm; T 9.3–12.5 cm

WEIGHT: 26–66 g

STATUS: Secure

BEHAVIOUR: This species is active at night, foraging on the ground and around tree trunks in open eucalypt forests and woodlands. If alarmed, it sometimes runs up trees and hides in a hollow. Breeding occurs for two weeks in late August and males die after mating.

THREATS: Feral cats, foxes, Dingoes and birds of prey.

Yellow-footed Antechinus *Antechinus flavipes*

This nimble antechinus is partly arboreal and darts along the underside of branches when in the treetops. On the ground, it forages in the leaf litter for insects and rodents.

DIET: Insects, small birds, rodents and nectar

LENGTH: HB 8.6–16.5 cm; T 6.5–15.1 cm

WEIGHT: 21–79 g

STATUS: Secure

BEHAVIOUR: These nocturnal marsupials are both arboreal and terrestrial. They are also gregarious and confident and have been known to enter houses. Breeding occurs only once a year, after which males die and females give birth to up to twelve young.

THREATS: Foxes, Dingoes, feral cats, dogs and birds of prey.

Southern Dibbler *Parantechinus apicalis*

First recorded in 1884, the Southern Dibbler vanished for more than 80 years until it was re-discovered in 1967 at Cheyne Beach, WA. It is still considered endangered on the mainland.

BEHAVIOUR: This species is nocturnal and only partly arboreal. In captivity they may breed twice yearly, but in the wild all males die after their first breeding season, which usually occurs in March.

THREATS: Foxes, feral cats, dogs, Dingoes and birds of prey.

DIET: Insects and possibly nectar

LENGTH: HB 14–14.5 cm; T 9.5–11.5 cm

WEIGHT: 40–100 g

STATUS: Endangered (Cmwth & IUCN Red List)

Sandstone Pseudantechinus
Pseudantechinus bilarni

Remarkably, this species only became known to scientists in 1948 because it is confined to the remote western Arnhem Land escarpment. Females have no pouch — young cling to the mother's teats.

BEHAVIOUR: The Sandstone Pseudantechinus is terrestrial and nocturnal, sheltering in cracks in quartz sandstone by day but sometimes emerging in the late afternoon to feed. Breeds once yearly; afterwards 75% of males die.

THREATS: Feral dogs, cats, Dingoes and birds of prey.

DIET: Insects and other small invertebrates

LENGTH: HB 9–11.5 cm; T 9–12.5 cm

WEIGHT: 15–40 g

STATUS: Secure

Fat-tailed Pseudantechinus
Pseudantechinus macdonellensis

The fat tail of this marsupial mammal is insurance against lean times — a common tactic in small dasyurids. When food is abundant, the tail becomes extremely thick.

BEHAVIOUR: This species is terrestrial and generally nocturnal, but may come out by day to bask on hot rocks in colder weather. It sometimes also lives in termites mounds. Each female has only one litter of up to six offspring each year.

THREATS: Dingoes, feral cats, dogs and birds of prey.

DIET: Insects and other small invertebrates

LENGTH: HB 9.5–10.5 cm; T 7.5–8.5 cm

WEIGHT: 20–45 g

STATUS: Secure

Mulgara *Dasycercus cristicauda*

Mulgaras are burrow-dwelling inhabitants of the sandy aridlands. They receive much of their water from their prey, which includes insects, spiders and some small vertebrates.

BEHAVIOUR: These fast, efficient hunters spend the hottest part of the day in burrows, some of which are quite complex. They are entirely terrestrial, solitary and nocturnal. Breeding probably occurs from May–Oct.

THREATS: Raptors, owls, feral cats, dogs, foxes and Dingoes.

DIET: Insects, spiders and small vertebrates
LENGTH: HB 12.5–22 cm; T 7.5–10 cm
WEIGHT: 60–170 g
STATUS: Vulnerable (Cmwth & IUCN Red List); Endangered (SA)

Kowari *Dasyuroides byrnei*

Both male and female Kowaris use scent glands on their chests and urinate to mark territory and the location of burrows. They fiercely defend their range, chattering and hissing at intruders.

BEHAVIOUR: Solitary and nocturnal, these mammals are entirely terrestrial. They make a number of vocalisations and twitch their tails (which terminate in a bushy black tip) when annoyed or threatened.

THREATS: Foxes, Dingoes, feral dogs, cats, raptors and owls.

DIET: Insects, carrion and small vertebrates
LENGTH: HB 13.5–18 cm; T 11–14 cm
WEIGHT: 70–140 g
STATUS: Vulnerable (IUCN Red List)

Brush-tailed Phascogale *Phascogale tapoatafa*

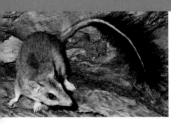

Brush-tailed Phascogales prefer dry eucalypt woodlands in coastal and hinterland regions of Australia where, unlike most dasyurids, they live an arboreal lifestyle.

BEHAVIOUR: Arboreal, nocturnal and gregarious. Males' home ranges overlap those of females. This species is an agile hunter of beetles, spiders and cockroaches and rarely hunts on the ground (although it has been known to kill and eat domestic fowl).

THREATS: Owls, foxes, cats, Dingoes, goannas and kookaburras.

DIET: Insects, spiders, small vertebrates, nectar
LENGTH: HB 14.8–26.1 cm; T 16–23.4 cm
WEIGHT: 106–311 g
STATUS: Vulnerable (NSW); Threatened (Vic); Endangered (SA)

Common Planigale *Planigale maculata*

Planigales are expert insect wranglers that ferociously attack prey larger than themselves.

BEHAVIOUR: The Common Planigale is nocturnal and mostly terrestrial in its favoured habitat of grasslands, marshes, forests and even suburban gardens. Females build nests of grass and have temporary pouches.

DIET: Insects
LENGTH: HB 7–10 cm; T 6.1–9.5 cm
WEIGHT: 6–22 g
STATUS: Vulnerable (NSW); Secure elsewhere

THREATS: Raptors, owls, feral cats, dogs and Dingoes.

Fat-tailed Dunnart *Sminthopsis crassicaudata*

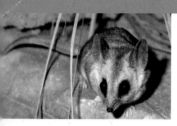

The Fat-tailed Dunnart does not need to drink and stores reserves of fat in its tail. During the day it shelters in nests beneath logs or rocks, or in cracks in the soil.

BEHAVIOUR: These large-eared marsupials are terrestrial, nocturnal and gregarious. By day they shelter in nests beneath logs or rocks, or within cracks in the soil. In cold weather, they huddle together in communal nests.

DIET: Invertebrates
LENGTH: HB 6–9 cm; T 4–7 cm
WEIGHT: 10–20 g
STATUS: Secure

THREATS: Foxes, feral cats, dogs, raptors, owls and Dingoes.

Little Long-tailed Dunnart
Sminthopsis dolichura

This species was once regarded as a subspecies of the Common Dunnart and was only given species status in 1984.

BEHAVIOUR: Hunts nocturnally, mostly in acacia and casuarina woodlands, for insects and rodents. Rests by day in grassy nests in hollow logs or within grass-trees as well as in deserted hopping-mice burrows. Males can breed at just 4–5 months. Females give birth once yearly.

DIET: Spiders, insects and geckoes
LENGTH: HB 6.3–9.9 cm; T 8.4–10.9 cm
WEIGHT: 10–21 g
STATUS: Secure

THREATS: Foxes, feral cats, owls, raptors, dogs and Dingoes.

Common Dunnart *Sminthopsis murina*

Populations of the Common Dunnart appear to flourish in the years following fire and it seems burning off of habitat and new-growth vegetation may benefit this species.

BEHAVIOUR: Nocturnal and solitary, Common Dunnarts rest by day in cup-shaped nests constructed of dried leaves and grass within hollow logs.

DIET: Insects and spiders
LENGTH: HB 6.4–10.4 cm; T 6.8–9.9 cm
WEIGHT: 10–28 g
STATUS: Secure

THREATS: Foxes, owls and cats. Often killed by Brown Antechinuses.

Stripe-faced Dunnart *Sminthopsis macroura*

The dark dorsal line running vertically down the forehead of this species gives it its common name. The tail, which is fat and longer than the body, is also a distinctive feature.

BEHAVIOUR: Probably entirely nocturnal. They don't appear to prefer a particular type of invertebrate prey. After rainfall, populations appear suddenly. They have the shortest gestation period of all marsupials (eleven days).

DIET: Invertebrates
LENGTH: HB 7–10 cm; T 8–11 cm
WEIGHT: 15–25 g
STATUS: Vulnerable (NSW); Secure elsewhere

THREATS: Soil erosion by domestic stock. Owls, foxes and cats.

Red-cheeked Dunnart *Sminthopsis virginiae*

There are two recognised Australian subspecies of the Red-cheeked Dunnart — virginiae and nitela. Both prefer savanna woodlands and subsist on insects and lizards.

BEHAVIOUR: Terrestrial and nocturnal, believed to nest on the ground beneath grass or pandanus fronds by day. Little is known about breeding in the wild.

DIET: Insects and small lizards
LENGTH: HB 9–13.5 cm; T 9–13.5 cm
WEIGHT: 18–58 g
STATUS: Secure

THREATS: Foxes, Dingoes, feral dogs, cats, owls and raptors.

Western Quoll *Dasyurus geoffroii*

Aborigines call this species the Chuditch in reference to the sound it makes. Like most of the quolls, its distribution has been reduced since European settlement and it is now severely restricted.

BEHAVIOUR: Although often seen in trees, the Western Quoll is mostly terrestrial and nests and lives on the ground. It is also usually nocturnal. Individuals have up to five dens in a 55–200 ha range.

THREATS: Foxes and raptors are predators.

DIET: Opportunistic — insects, ground-nesting birds, carrion, small mammals, invertebrates

LENGTH: HB 26–40 cm; T 21–35 cm

WEIGHT: 600–2200 g

STATUS: Vulnerable (Cmwth & IUCN); Extinct (NSW); Endangered (SA); Vulnerable (NT)

Northern Quoll *Dasyurus hallucatus*

Although the smallest of the quolls, the Northern Quoll is also the most ferocious. Its range has declined, probably due to poisoning when attempting to eat the toxic Cane Toad.

BEHAVIOUR: This is the most arboreal quoll and dens in hollow tree trunks. Males die after breeding season. Both sexes have been reported to have a highly "pugnacious disposition".

THREATS: Cane Toads, competition with feral cats, foxes and Dingoes.

DIET: Opportunistic — insects, invertebrates, reptiles, small mammals, ground-nesting birds, carrion and fruits

LENGTH: HB 12–31 cm; T 12–30 cm

WEIGHT: 300–900 g

STATUS: Near Threatened (IUCN Red List & NT)

The Eastern Quoll once enjoyed a wide range from eastern NSW to south-east SA, but it experienced a rapid decline at the beginning of the 20th century and is now confined to Tasmania. Although believed extinct on the mainland, reported sightings of this quoll have recently resurfaced in NSW.

FEATURES: Distinguished from the slightly larger Spotted-tail Quoll by colour (the Eastern Quoll is usually paler), its lack of tail spots and also the number of hindfoot digits (four). Its soft, dense, fawn fur has scattered spots and its large ears are rounded.

DIET & HABITAT: The Eastern Quoll occupies diverse habitats including coastal heath, dry eucalypt forests, scrublands and farmlands. Its preference seems to be areas where forest intersects pastures. In some areas, it is welcomed by graziers because it feeds on agricultural pests. Insects comprise most of its diet, which is supplemented by other small mammals, such as rabbits, rodents, bandicoots and ground-nesting birds, as well as carrion and fruit.

BEHAVIOUR: Mostly terrestrial and nocturnal. Individuals are solitary, occupying small, but overlapping, home ranges. At night, males forage up to 1 km from their dens but females stay within a few hundred metres of the den. Females sometime share dens.

BREEDING: Mating occurs from May–June and females give birth to 6 mm long immature young after a gestation period of 21 days. Females develop a temporary "flap" pouch where young suckle until they weigh about 20 g. After this time, they stay in a den until independent at eleven months of age.

THREATS: May fall prey to, and compete with, feral cats, foxes and dogs. Land clearing is a threat.

Above, left to right: Eastern Quolls forage in the undergrowth for fruit, insects and rodents, but also take larger vertebrate prey such as birds and other small mammals; A nest of baby quolls bred in captivity. Female Eastern Quolls can have as many as 30 offspring in a litter, but have only six nipples.

DIET: Opportunistic — insects, invertebrates, ground-nesting birds, small mammals and carrion

LENGTH: HB 28–45 cm; T 17–28 cm

WEIGHT: 700–2000 g

STATUS: Secure (Tas); Endangered/Extinct (mainland)

Impossible to confuse with any of the other marsupials that share its order, the unique Numbat is the sole living member of the family Myrmecobiidae and is the faunal emblem of WA. It is also a specialist termite eater, using its strong olfactory sense to sniff out termite mounds and devour the insects within by flicking out its extremely long tongue. Like most members of the Dasyuromorphia order, the Numbat's distribution has decreased significantly since European occupation of Australia.

FEATURES: The Numbat's long, bushy tail, banded rump and "masked" eye patch make it a highly distinctive species and one of the most attractive and colourful animals within its order. A remarkable feature is its extra-long tongue. The Numbat's hindfoot has only four toes, as it is terrestrial.

DIET & HABITAT: Numbats are now restricted to small areas of Wandoo, Powderbark and Jarrah eucalypt forest in South-West WA. These environments have a high distribution of termite mounds and provide plenty of shelter in the form of hollow logs and fallen branches.

BEHAVIOUR: Numbats are mostly solitary and diurnal, hunting by day when termites are most active and easily captured. Individuals occupy home territories; however, these may overlap with territories that belong to members of the opposite sex. Numbats sleep and nest in hollow logs but may also burrow and build a nest chamber during winter.

BREEDING: Females breed in January and give birth two weeks later. They have only four teats and no pouch; instead, the young hang from the teats until the end of July when they are left in a nursery burrow and suckled nightly until fully weaned in October. They are independent at around ten months.

THREATS: Little Eagles, Brown Goshawks, Collared Sparrowhawks, Wedge-tailed Eagles, Carpet Pythons and foxes are known predators. Recovery programs for this species are underway in WA.

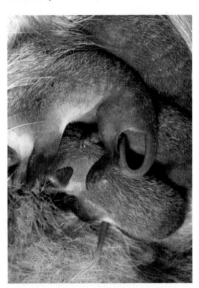

Above: Females have no pouch, so young nestle into the hair on the mother's belly and cling on to a teat. **Opposite, top to bottom:** Following a termite trail; The colourful Numbat.

DIET: Exists solely on termites and some ant species

LENGTH: HB 20–27.4 cm; T 16.1–21 cm

WEIGHT: 300–715 g

STATUS: Vulnerable (Cmwth & IUCN Red List)

Until it became protected in 1941, the Tasmanian Devil was hunted almost to the brink of extinction. In the past, this species had a somewhat undeserved reputation for savagery. Devils mostly only hunt insects, birds and small to medium-sized mammals. Most of the larger animals they are seen devouring are either carrion left over from roadkill or the remains of prey killed by larger carnivorous predators (such as Dingoes and foxes). The Tassie Devil's bad name was probably a result of its growling, shrieking and squabbling over carcasses; such behaviour, however, is mostly bravado.

FEATURES: The Tasmanian Devil is stout, well-muscled and about the size of a medium dog. It has glossy black fur and a white band on the chest. There is often also a white band at the base of the tail, as well as a white patch on the underarm. The ears are small and rounded and become red and engorged with blood when the animal is stressed or upset. Tasmanian Devils have five toes on each forepaw and four on each hindpaw. Males are larger than females and have a thicker neck. Both sexes have a large, toothy gape and powerful jaws.

DIET & HABITAT: Tasmanian Devils probably became extinct on the mainland about 400 years ago. They have few predators in Tasmania and are not very selective about either habitat or diet. They are found in woodlands, heathlands, farmlands, and eucalypt forests where they feed on insects, small mammals (generally smaller than themselves) and carrion.

BEHAVIOUR: Tasmanian Devils are entirely terrestrial and solitary, occupying home ranges of about 10–20 ha, which overlap with the ranges of other Tasmanian Devils. In a single night, these marsupials may cover up to 16 km while searching for food.

BREEDING: Mating occurs in March. Females have a backwards-facing pouch in which they suckle two to four offspring for fifteen weeks. After this time, the juveniles remain in the den.

THREATS: Recently this species has been threatened by the cancerous Devil Facial Tumour Disease.

Above: A mother and her young plunder a carcass. **Right, clockwise from top:** Fighting over a meal is common; Devils have a keen sense of smell; "Gaping" helps deter threats.

DIET: Insects, small mammals, birds and carrion

LENGTH: HB 57–65 cm; T 24.5–26 cm
WEIGHT: 7–9 kg
STATUS: Secure

Bilby & Bandicoots

The Bilby has recently raised its profile by becoming the Australian substitute for the "Easter Bunny". In fact, this small marsupial has little in common with rabbits save for its long ears and tendency to burrow. Its true relatives are Australia's seven bandicoot species, and it shares the order Peramelemorphia and the family Peramelidae with all but one of them. The exception is the Rufous Spiny Bandicoot — the sole Australian member of the family Peroryctidae. Bandicoots are unlike most other marsupials. Developing embryos are attached to a placenta in the womb; however, this placenta does not nourish the young. Females also have a backwards-facing pouch.

Bilby *Macrotis lagotis*

Australia was once home to two species of these burrowing marsupials, but the smaller of the two, the Lesser Bilby, has not been sighted since 1931 and is now considered extinct. The Bilby's long ears are a useful adaptation for desert life. Bilbies do not need to drink and cannot sweat; instead, blood vessels situated close to the skin's surface allow excess heat to dissipate from the ears.

FEATURES: Silvery to blue-grey body fur with buff or fawn on the flanks and cheeks and a creamy white underbelly. The pointed face is topped with long, pink ears and the black, crested tail has a white tip.

DIET & HABITAT: The Bilby is perfectly adapted for life in the Gibson, Tanami and Great Sandy Deserts where it thrives on insects, seeds, fungi, bulbs and fruit.

BEHAVIOUR: Bilbies are wholly terrestrial and nocturnal, sheltering in a burrow by day and feeding at night.

BREEDING: They breed year round. Females have eight nipples but give birth to just one or two offspring each litter. Baby Bilbies spend 75–80 days in the pouch.

THREATS: Dingoes, foxes, feral cats and competition with rabbits.

Top to bottom: Bilby; Bilbies maintain several burrows within their range.

DIET: Insects (particularly witchetty grubs), seeds, bulbs (especially wild onion), grasses, fungi and fruit

LENGTH: HB 29–55 cm; T 20–29 cm
WEIGHT: 800–2500 g
STATUS: Vulnerable (Cmwth & IUCN Red List)

Rufous Spiny Bandicoot *Echymipera rufescens*

The Rufous Spiny Bandicoot is the only rainforest-dwelling native bandicoot and most likely evolved from a Melanesian species that was isolated in Australia in the Late Pleistocene.

BEHAVIOUR: The Rufous Spiny Bandicoot is terrestrial and nocturnal, moving around the rainforest at night to feed on an omnivorous diet of insects and vegetation. Males are much larger than females.

THREATS: Dingoes, feral cats, habitat destruction and clearing.

DIET: Little known but believed to be omnivorous
LENGTH: HB 30–40 cm; T 7.5–10 cm
WEIGHT: 0.5–2 kg
STATUS: Secure

Golden Bandicoot *Isoodon auratus*

This species was first described in 1887, but European settlement has drastically reduced its mainland range and it is now most abundant on Barrow Island off the WA coast.

BEHAVIOUR: Like most bandicoots, this species is very territorial within its solitary home range. They are nocturnal and in arid areas shelter by day in grass nests, caves and tussocks of spinifex.

THREATS: Feral cats, Dingoes and habitat damage due to stock.

DIET: Insects, roots, tubers, small mammals, reptiles and turtle eggs
LENGTH: HB 19–29.5 cm; T 8.4–12.1 cm
WEIGHT: 250–670 g
STATUS: Vulnerable (IUCN Red List); Endangered (SA & NT)

Southern Brown Bandicoot *Isoodon obesulus*

Burning off of ground cover appears to benefit this species, which can breed very rapidly when food is plentiful. Despite this, it remains endangered on the mainland.

BEHAVIOUR: This ground-living species aggressively defends a home range of 2–7 ha. They are solitary, nocturnal and somewhat timid, rarely venturing far from cover even when foraging.

THREATS: Mortality is high in juveniles, and territory is difficult to come by. Foxes, Dingoes and feral cats are their main predators.

DIET: Insects, roots, tubers, small mammals and reptiles
LENGTH: HB 30–36 cm; T 9–14 cm
WEIGHT: 400–1600 g
STATUS: Vulnerable (SA)

Western Barred Bandicoot *Perameles bougainville*

This bandicoot has also suffered adversely since the arrival of Europeans in Australia. It once occupied a much wider range but is now restricted to Bernier and Dorre Islands off WA.

BEHAVIOUR: The Western Barred Bandicoot is solitary and nocturnal, resting during the day in grassy nests (concealed in a hollow beneath a fallen log) and foraging at dusk. Adults never share nests with other adults.

THREATS: Predation by owls and, for juveniles, monitor lizards.

DIET: Insects, seeds, roots, herbs and leaves

LENGTH: HB 17.1–23.6 cm; T 6–10.2 cm

WEIGHT: 172–286 g

STATUS: Endangered (IUCN Red List)

Eastern Barred Bandicoot *Perameles gunnii*

Eastern Barred Bandicoots have a characteristic galloping gait and three or four prominent "bars" or bands across the rump that make this species easy to identify.

BEHAVIOUR: This species is terrestrial and nocturnal, sleeping by day in a grassy nest. The Eastern Barred Bandicoot uses its clawed forepaws to excavate long, conical holes into which it pokes its snout to search for insects, insect larvae, bulbs and tubers.

THREATS: Foxes on the mainland. Owls, feral cats, Dingoes and dogs.

DIET: Insects, worms, larvae, bulbs, tubers, fruit

LENGTH: HB 27–35 cm; T 7–11 cm

WEIGHT: 500–1450 g

STATUS: Endangered (SA); Threatened (Vic); Vulnerable (IUCN Red List)

Long-nosed Bandicoot *Perameles nasuta*

All bandicoots have long noses, but this species has the longest and is renowned for digging long, conical tunnels in backyards and fields along Australia's east coast.

BEHAVIOUR: Days are spent in a grass- and leaf-lined nest that is vacated at night to forage. Long-nosed Bandicoots are terrestrial, territorial and highly solitary, with males and females coming together only to mate.

THREATS: Foxes, Dingoes, feral dogs, cats and birds of prey.

DIET: Roots and tubers, vegetation, insects and their larvae

LENGTH: HB 31–42.5 cm; T 12–15.5 cm

WEIGHT: 850–1100 g

STATUS: Secure

Marsupial Moles

Australia's two marsupial mole species are the most rarely observed and mysterious of Australia's marsupials. In 1888, they were wrongly classified as monotremes, but they are marsupials and, while there is still much conjecture over their correct classification, it is probable that they represent a unique evolutionary lineage that dates back at least 50 million years. Their similarity to the African Golden Mole (a placental mammal) seems to be a remarkable reminder of convergent evolution, as they do not share ancestry. Both Australian species are blind and earless, with the Northern Marsupial Mole (*Notoryctes caurinus*) being slightly smaller than its southern kin.

Southern Marsupial Mole *Notoryctes typhlops*

Aborigines called this marsupial mole "Itjari-itjari" and used to trade its soft, silky pelt to cameleers and settlers in the early days of settlement. When these moles come to the surface following rain, they leave distinctive tracks that divulge their presence to Indigenous hunters. Marsupial mole fossils from up to 15–20 million years ago have been found in north-west Queensland.

FEATURES: The Southern Marsupial Mole's silky fur can be anything from a pinkish white to a deep golden colour. It is entirely blind, with ears that are just tiny holes protected from the sand by a covering of long hair. The body terminates in a stub-like tail. All feet have five toes, although two of the front toes are specially adapted for tunnelling through sand and are long, flattened and spade-like. A tough, shield-like patch of skin covers the nose. Males may have a poorly developed pouch.

DIET & HABITAT: Marsupial moles travel through horizontal tunnels 100–200 m long. These are built below the sandy surface of deserts that have a top covering of spinifex and Mulga. They are carnivores that feed on insect larvae and beetles.

BEHAVIOUR: Marsupial moles are most likely solitary creatures that enjoy a subterranean and terrestrial lifestyle. Generally, these animals only come to the surface following rain, although animals in captivity regularly feed above the ground.

BREEDING: Females have a backwards-facing pouch that contains two teats, but their breeding biology is largely unknown.

THREATS: Because of its reclusive nature, little is known about how abundant this marsupial is in the wild. Aborigines used to hunt marsupial moles, and it is also likely that they are occasionally preyed upon by Dingoes, foxes and feral cats.

DIET: Insects and their larvae

LENGTH: HB 12.1–15.9 cm; T 2.1–2.6 cm
WEIGHT: 40–70 g
STATUS: Endangered

The order Diprodontia is highly successful and contains Australia's most familiar and iconic mammals — all widely diverse in form (and occupying different suborders) but sharing some common characteristics.

Firstly, all of these marsupials are regarded as largely herbivorous (in contrast with the smaller, carnivorous dasyurids and omnivorous bandicoots); however, a few of them also eat insects and sap or nectar on occasion. Despite this deviation, the order name is derived from their specialist herbivorous dentition and translates from Greek as "two front teeth" — a reference to the fact that they have only one pair of lower incisors. Members of this order also lack lower canine teeth, which are unnecessary for grazing and browsing animals. Secondly, they are distinguished by their feet and toes. Like the bandicoots, the second and third toes on the hindfoot are partly fused, giving diprotodonts a "grooming" toe that is used to untangle matted fur. Some arboreal individuals, such as the Koala and ringtail possums, also possess opposable digits on the forelimbs; aside from primates, they are the only mammals to enjoy this dexterity.

Within the order are two suborders, the Vombatiformes (including the Koala and wombats) and the larger Phalangerida (which contains all of the possums and kangaroos separated into different superfamilies).

Above: Koalas are unique marsupials that are related to the terrestrial wombat, with which they share a suborder.
Right: Kangaroos and wallabies belong to the large superfamily Macropodoidea.

Northern Hairy-nosed Wombat *Lasiorhinus krefftii*

With a range of just 300 ha in Epping Forest National Park, Qld, this wombat is critically endangered and was at one time considered to be extinct. Its wild population hovers at around 118 individuals.

BEHAVIOUR: Northern Hairy-nosed Wombats are terrestrial and solitary within a small home range, but they may share burrows.

THREATS: Fire, drought, encroachment of unpalatable buffel grass upon their foraging areas. Conservation programs are in place.

DIET: Native grasses, forbs (teeth grow continuously)

LENGTH: HB 97.1–110.6 cm; T 5 cm

WEIGHT: 26.9–35.1 kg

STATUS: Critically Endangered (IUCN Red List)

Southern Hairy-nosed Wombat
Lasiorhinus latifrons

Both species of hairy-nosed wombat belong to a separate genus from the Common Wombat. They are distinguished by their hairy noses, longer, pointy ears and squarer snouts. Both species have declined greatly in range.

BEHAVIOUR: These sedentary, nocturnal marsupials spend 3–8 hours each night foraging. By day, they sleep in burrow networks that may house five to ten wombats.

THREATS: Competition with rabbits/stock degrades feeding areas.

DIET: Native grasses and forbs (especially wallaby grass and kangaroo grass)

LENGTH: HB 77.2–93.4 cm; T 2.5–6 cm

WEIGHT: 19–32 kg

STATUS: Endangered (NSW); Secure (SA)

Common Wombat *Vombatus ursinus*

Common Wombats are the largest burrowing marsupials on Earth. There are three subspecies (V. u. ursinus, V. u. tasmaniensis and V. u. hirsutus). Early settlers referred to them, incorrectly, as "badgers".

BEHAVIOUR: Visits up to four burrows daily within a home range of 5–23 ha. They are nocturnal in summer, but may be seen feeding by day in winter. In overlapping ranges, burrows may be shared.

THREATS: Competition with rabbits/stock and habitat clearing.

DIET: Native grasses, sedges, roots of trees and shrubs

LENGTH: HB 90– 115 cm; T 2.5 cm

WEIGHT: 22–39 kg

STATUS: Rare (Qld & SA); Secure elsewhere

Unsurprisingly, given its teddy-bear-like appearance, the Koala is one of the nation's most beloved marsupials. However, due to its excellent camouflage in the treetops and slow-moving, somnambulant lifestyle, it is seldom seen in the wild and is mostly encountered by the public at wildlife parks. This species was the unfortunate victim of widespread trapping campaigns in the late 1800s, when as many as 300,000 pelts per year were exported to England. Koalas eventually became protected in the late 1920s, but not before they suffered a devastating decline in numbers.

FEATURES: The Koala is unmistakable, with dense grey fur, rounded furry ears and an oval black nose. White spots on the bottom and a creamy underbelly camouflage Koalas in the dappled treetops when observed from below. Colour and size varies; southern populations are darker, fluffier and larger than those in the north. Males have a dark patch of fur around a scent gland on the chest. Koalas are the only arboreal marsupials to lack a tail.

DIET & HABITAT: Koalas are specialised gum leaf eaters and are found only in areas where particular "food tree" eucalypts are plentiful. Preferred trees vary with the Koala's distribution. Eating eucalypt leaves allows Koalas to exploit a niche diet. The leaves are toxic, but Koalas are able to digest them safely by choosing young (less toxic) leaves

and digesting them with the aid of a long caecum (similar to the human appendix). This diet is high in fibre and not very nutritious, which is why Koalas have such a slow metabolism and remain inactive for twenty hours a day.

BEHAVIOUR: Individuals vigorously defend "home trees" within a territory but may come into contact with others in shared "food trees" within overlapping ranges. They communicate via grunts (bellows) and scenting.

BREEDING: Mates from Sept–Feb. One joey is born after 35 days gestation and is nurtured on milk and then on faecal "pap" to introduce its gut to micro-organisms needed for a gum leaf diet.

THREATS: Wild dogs. Chlamydia causes pneumonia and infertility. Clearing of eucalypts is highly detrimental.

Above: The male's sternal gland is used to scent trees within is territory, leaving a Koala "calling card" to warn other males and attract females. When they reach maturity, males and females must find their own home range.

DIET: Eucalypt leaves, such as River Red Gum, Blue Gum, Swamp Gum, Manna Gum, Tallowwood and Grey Gum (among others)

LENGTH: HB 64.8–82 cm; T absent
WEIGHT: 4.1–14.9 kg
STATUS: Rare (SA, NT & IUCN Red List); Vulnerable (NSW)

Top left: When they are not sleeping, Koalas spend their time grooming or carefully choosing eucalypt leaves. They are notoriously fussy eaters, selecting only tender leaves and shoots that are low in toxins and higher in water content. The name Koala is derived from an Aboriginal word meaning "no drink", because Koalas drink only during drought. **Top right:** The denser, darker fur of southern individuals helps insulate them in a cooler climate. **Above:** Joeys (the correct term for baby Koalas) are sometimes abandoned by their mothers if they fall from the treetops. They may also become casualties of their mother's death on the roads. These orphaned joeys, when discovered, are frequently raised by dedicated carers in wildlife parks. **Left:** Koalas rarely come to ground, where they are vulnerable to attack.

Possums & Gliders

Possums and their relatives fall into one of four superfamilies, which can be further divided into six family groups. Pygmy-possums belong to the family Burramyidae, while the larger brushtail possums, cuscuses and Scaly-tailed Possum are members of the family Phalangeridae. Ringtail possums share some features with the large Greater Glider, which occupies the family Pseudocheiridae with them. The other gliders, known as wrist-winged gliders (such as the Sugar Glider) and the Striped and Leadbeater's Possum are grouped in the family Petauridae, while the Honey Possum and Feathertail Glider are sole members of the families Tarsipedidae and Acrobatidae respectively. Some authorities disagree with the classification of some possum species into these separate families.

Mountain Pygmy-possum *Burramys parvus*

This pygmy-possum was recorded in 1895 from fossil remains, but only found living in 1966. It is the only Australian mammal to occupy an alpine–subalpine range and the only native mammal to hibernate for prolonged periods.

DIET: Arthropods, Bogong Moths, seeds, fruit of Snow-beard Heath and Plum Pine

LENGTH: HB 11–13.8 cm; T 13.6–13.8 cm

WEIGHT: 30–82 g

STATUS: Threatened (Vic); Endangered (IUCN Red List)

BEHAVIOUR: Mountain Pygmy-possums are nocturnal and terrestrial. They roll into balls and hibernate for up to seven months, decreasing their metabolic rate by 98%. They store seeds to consume later.

THREATS: Feral predators, Dingoes, global warming and habitat loss.

Long-tailed Pygmy-possum
Cercartetus caudatus

Australia's only rainforest pygmy-possum, the Long-tailed Pygmy-possum inhabits areas between Townsville and Cooktown, where it is sometimes confused with the Prehensile-tailed Rat (a rodent), which shares its range.

DIET: Nectar and insects

LENGTH: HB 10.3–10.8 cm; T 12.8–15.1 cm

WEIGHT: 25–40 g

STATUS: Secure in limited habitat

BEHAVIOUR: Nocturnal and arboreal, using its prehensile tail to grasp branches. Builds a spherical nest in tree stumps or amid fern fronds. May enter torpor in cool weather. Makes "sik-sik" distress calls.

THREATS: Owls, pythons, Spotted-tailed Quolls and deforestation.

Western Pygmy-possum *Cercartetus concinnus*

This tiny species is a prolific breeder, which thankfully counteracts a high-level of predation by cats. It sleeps deeply by day, curling itself up and covering its eyes with its large, thin ears.

BEHAVIOUR: This is a nimble, nocturnal species that is seldom seen unless captured asleep in its gum leaf nest within tree stumps, grass-trees or abandoned birds' nests.

THREATS: Cats, foxes, Dingoes, land clearing and development.

DIET: Insects and nectar, grasping food in hand-like forepaws

LENGTH: HB 7.1–10.6 cm; T 7.1–9.6 cm

WEIGHT: 8–20 g

STATUS: Endangered (NSW); Secure elsewhere

Little Pygmy-possum *Cercartetus lepidus*

At just 6 g, this is the smallest of the continent's possums. It is an adept climber with a prehensile tail, but prefers to dwell in shrubs close to the ground, where it will undergo torpor if needed.

BEHAVIOUR: A nocturnal and secretive species, little is known about its behaviour. It makes a nest in logs or stumps and sometimes in ploughed fields or disused birds' nests. May go into torpor for up to six days in cold weather.

THREATS: Dingoes, cats, carnivorous mammals, snakes and owls.

DIET: Arthropods, reptiles, some nectar

LENGTH: HB 5–6.5 cm; T 6–7.5 cm

WEIGHT: 6–9 g

STATUS: Secure

Eastern Pygmy-possum *Cercartetus nanus*

The Eastern Pygmy-possum has a specialised brush-tipped tongue for lapping nectar, although it also feeds on insects and soft fruit.

BEHAVIOUR: These possums are tiny and terrestrial, sheltering by day in tree hollows. Nests seem to be built only by breeding females. They are generally silent but sometimes hiss if upset. They spend winter in torpor.

THREATS: Carnivorous mammals, owls, snakes, habitat loss.

DIET: Nectar, pollen, fruit, insects and spiders

LENGTH: HB 7–11 cm; T 7.5–10.5 cm

WEIGHT: 15–43 g

STATUS: Vulnerable (NSW & SA); Secure elsewhere

Initially, all ringtail possum species were classified in the family Petauridae with the wrist-winged gliders and their relatives; however, they are now considered sufficiently different to be placed in their own family, which they share only with the Greater Glider. As the name implies, the Common Ringtail Possum is the most widely distributed ringtail and is often seen in suburban areas along the east coast of the continent. There are four recognised subspecies (P. p. peregrinus, P. p. cookii, P. p. convolutor and P. p. pulcher).

FEATURES: Colour varies widely, from a rufous-brown to charcoal on the back and a cream to white underbelly. The thin, prehensile tail has a white tip and is used as a fifth limb for moving about the treetops (a furless textured strip on the underside increases traction). Extra grip is provided by syndactylus fingers on the forepaws. The ears are short and rounded with a white patch behind.

DIET & HABITAT: Diverse, from suburban gardens to rainforests, woodlands, eucalypt forests and coastal shrublands where they eat fruit, leaves and flowers. They are particularly fond of rosebuds. Common Ringtails are one of the few possums to eat gum leaves.

BEHAVIOUR: These nocturnal marsupials feed and groom in early evening, before resting and returning to foraging before dawn. They sleep in nests lined with torn up bark and leaves, usually in tree hollows or in thick vegetation near the ground. Common Ringtail Possums are sociable animals, with small family groups sharing nests and feeding areas.

BREEDING: Pairs usually bond for more than one season, but males may mate with other females too. Breeding is from Apr–Nov and two offspring are produced. They remain in the mother's pouch for four months, after which both sexes may piggyback and care for young (a trait unique among possums).

THREATS: Cats and foxes are probably major predators. Habitat destruction.

Above: The second and first fingers of the Common Ringtail's forepaws are syndactylous (able to be brought together) to give them a better grip on food and tree limbs.

DIET: Leaves, flowers and fruits; able to eat gum leaves; eats own faeces in the nest

LENGTH: HB 30–35 cm; T 30–35 cm
WEIGHT: 700–1100 g
STATUS: Secure

Top left: Common Ringtails are nocturnal but may be seen resting in the treetops by day and venturing out in the early evening to feed around campsites and picnic grounds. **Top right:** Some individuals are reddish in colour with a highly contrasting white underbelly, while others are darker, becoming almost black on the upper side of the body. **Above:** Common Ringtails have become quite accustomed to humans, with whom they share most of their range along Australia's heavily developed eastern seaboard. Many are frequent visitors to backyard fruit trees and orchards, as well as native plants in parks and gardens — some even regard suburban verandas as part of their range. **Left:** A nest box in a suburban eucalypt provides a secure spot for a daytime nap.

Lemuroid Ringtail Possum *Hemibelideus lemuroides*

Lemuroid Ringtail Possums are extremely nimble in the treetops and may leap and freefall distances of 2–3 m in their arboreal abode.

BEHAVIOUR: Nocturnal and strictly tree-living, Lemuroid Ringtail Possums are often seen in small family groups, and up to eight may gather to feed. They forage at night and remain active until dawn. Juveniles make squeaky, high-pitched distress calls; adults are silent.

THREATS: Carpet Pythons and deforestation.

DIET: Folivores that feed mainly on Queensland Maple, Brown Quandong and Tamarind leaves; also some flowers and fruit

LENGTH: HB 31.3– 40 cm; T 30–37.3 cm

WEIGHT: 750–1060 g

STATUS: Rare (NSW); Near Threatened (IUCN Red List)

Rock Ringtail Possum *Petropseudes dahli*

Aborigines first brought this species to scientific attention in 1895, but until a specimen was found it was believed to be a type of tree-kangaroo. This species is secretive and, unlike most ringtail possums, does not build a nest.

BEHAVIOUR: Rock Ringtail Possums are nocturnal and semi-terrestrial, hiding in crevices by day and feeding by night. They are sociable but territorial and communicate by scenting.

THREATS: Olive Pythons and Dingoes. Human intrusion.

DIET: Blossoms and fruit (particularly Darwin Woollybutt, Stringybark and Billy Goat Plums)

LENGTH: HB 33.4– 38.3 cm; T 20–26 cm

WEIGHT: 1280–2000 g

STATUS: Secure

Western Ringtail Possum *Pseudocheirus occidentalis*

Predation by foxes has most likely caused the decline of Western Ringtail Possums, which are now restricted to a small range in the south-western tip of WA.

BEHAVIOUR: This species is strongly arboreal and seldom leaves the canopy. Adults are solitary and move from drey to drey, occupying up to eight hollows a year in overlapping home ranges. At night they follow scent trails and are quite social.

THREATS: Foxes and habitat destruction.

DIET: Mainly the leaves of Peppermint trees, but also Marri and Jarrah leaves

LENGTH: HB 30– 40 cm; T 30–40 cm

WEIGHT: 900–1100 g

STATUS: Vulnerable (IUCN Red List); Rare (WA)

Green Ringtail Possum *Pseudochirops archeri*

The Green Ringtail Possum is superbly camouflaged in the rainforest canopy thanks to the combination of black, white and yellow banded hairs that give this possum its overall moss-green appearance.

BEHAVIOUR: The Green Ringtail Possum is solitary and arboreal, coming down only to move between trees. It is the only possum known to dine on the leaves of fig trees and has a highly specialised diet.

THREATS: Spotted-tailed Quolls, owls and logging.

DIET: Foliage of fig trees, Kurrajong, oaks and Rose Maple

LENGTH: HB 28.5– 37.1 cm; T 30.9–37.2 cm

WEIGHT: 670–1350 g

STATUS: Near Threatened (IUCN Red List); Rare (Qld)

In 1945, this species was first described as a subspecies of the Herbert River Ringtail Possum. It was only in 1989 that scientists discovered it was a distinct species with sixteen pairs of chromosomes (compared with the Herbert River Ringtail's twelve chromosomes).

Above: Daintree River Ringtails seldom make large, daring leaps between branches, preferring to climb carefully from limb to limb.

FEATURES: Similar in appearance to the Herbert River Ringtail. The upper body is a light caramel to brown with a creamy coloured underside. A long, dark stripe extends from the forehead down the spine to the lower back. The tail has a white tip and a bare patch of skin on the underside to aid grip. Juveniles are paler than adults.

DIET & HABITAT: Three distinct populations exist in the highland rainforest of Mount Windsor Tableland, Mount Carbine Tableland and Thornton Peak in north Queensland. Here, they feed in the canopy on the leaves of rainforest trees and fruit. Green-leaved Moreton Bay Figs have been recorded as favourites during the spring.

BEHAVIOUR: They are arboreal and nocturnal, presumably spending the day in tree hollows, although some are also seen sleeping on tree limbs. Individuals are solitary, most likely only coming together to court and mate. When disturbed, they vocalise with hissing, grunts and "sik-sik" sounds.

BREEDING: Further investigation into breeding behaviour is required, but it is probably similar to that of the Herbert River Ringtail. It appears that the breeding season is extended, but with a peak in Apr–May. Females have two teats in the pouch and are thought to raise two joeys after each mating.

THREATS: Juveniles are preyed upon by the Spotted-tailed Quoll, Lesser Sooty Owl, Dingo and pythons.

DIET: Leaves and fruits of rainforest plants

LENGTH: HB 33.5–36.8 cm; T 32–39.5 cm
WEIGHT: 700–1450 g
STATUS: Rare (Qld); Near Threatened (IUCN Red List)

Thankfully, most of the Herbert River Ringtail's prime habitat is now safeguarded within the Wet Tropics World Heritage Area of north Queensland. Were this not the case, the species could be in danger because populations appear to be drastically reduced in pockets of rainforest less than 20 ha in size.

FEATURES: Bulging red eyes, rimmed with white, are a distinctive feature. Adults are mostly dark brown to black with varying degrees of white on the belly, chest and forelimbs. The ears are smaller than those of the Daintree River Ringtail, although the long, tapered tail sports a similar white tip.

DIET & HABITAT: Occupies tropical rainforest above 350 m altitude and adjoining eucalypt forest around the Herbert River. They feed mostly on the foliage of rainforest plants, choosing high-protein leaves.

BEHAVIOUR: They emerge after dark, grooming for an hour before foraging. By day, they rest in hollows or epiphytic ferns. Although solitary, males may follow females for days before mating.

BREEDING: Extended mating period. Females produce two young from May–July and offspring stay in the pouch for 105–120 days.

THREATS: Carpet Pythons, owls and deforestation are the main threats.

Above: Once young Herbert River Ringtails vacate the nest, they cling to their mother's back for a further two weeks. Most other possums remain on their mother's back for a much longer period. Juvenile Herbert River Ringtails are relatively pale, resembling the Daintree River Ringtail in colour.

DIET: High-protein leaves of rainforest plants, including Pink Ash, Paperbark Satinash and the fruits of the Silver Quandong (among others)

LENGTH: HB 30.1–40 cm; T 29–47 cm
WEIGHT: 800–1530 g
STATUS: Near Threatened (IUCN Red List); Rare (Qld)

The Greater Glider differs from other gliders in a few major ways. As its name suggests, it is the largest glider (being three times larger than the Yellow-bellied Glider). The Greater Glider is also the only glider to share the same family as the ringtail possums (Pseudocheiridae) — a distinction made because the gliding membranes on its arms reach only to its elbows, not to its wrists, as do the membranes of the wrist-winged gliders in the family Petauridae.

FEATURES: Individuals may be grey to mottled cream or a darker brown, with a creamy white underside. The head and tail are sometimes paler in colour than the body. Greater Gliders don't have a prehensile tail. The eyes are large and somewhat bugged, and the ears are often fringed with fluffy fur.

DIET & HABITAT: Eucalypt leaves sustain Greater Gliders, which possess a large caecum to help them break down the cellulose contained in gum leaves. They inhabit areas where eucalypts are plentiful along Australia's east coast, but generally feed on only one or two eucalypt species in each area.

BEHAVIOUR: These gliders are highly arboreal, nocturnal and solitary.

BREEDING: Breeding occurs Mar–June, and females have one offspring that remains in the pouch for 3–4 months.

THREATS: Deforestation, particularly of old-growth forests.

Above: Greater Gliders volplane, or glide, using a thin membrane of skin (the patagium) that stretches from the elbow to the ankle along each side of the body. When the limbs are not extended, the membrane is hard to see.

DIET: Foliage of eucalypts

LENGTH: HB 35–45 cm; T 45–60 cm
WEIGHT: 900–1700 g
STATUS: Secure

Yellow-bellied Glider *Petaurus australis*

The next largest glider species is the Yellow-bellied Glider, which has the longest, fluffiest tail of all the gliders. It is a wrist-winged glider and is able to glide remarkable distances (up to 150 m). These gliders are also highly sociable and live in hierarchical family groups controlled by a dominant male that marks his kin with his own scent in order to recognise them.

FEATURES: Colour may be pale grey to dark charcoal. Underbelly also varies from cream to yellow or white and is mostly paler on juveniles. The base of the tail and limbs are black with white claws and gliding membranes attached from wrists to ankles. The face is short with large, furless ears.

DIET & HABITAT: Yellow-bellied Gliders chew V-shaped notches in the bark of gum trees and lick and suck up the sap. They dwell in eucalypt woodlands feeding on pollen and nectar.

BEHAVIOUR: This species is noisy, gregarious and nocturnal, resting by day in tree hollows. Grooming is performed while hanging head-down from a branch.

BREEDING: Offspring is born Aug–Sept, and although females have two teats, each in their own compartment of the pouch, they seldom have twins. Offspring remains in the pouch for around 100 days.

THREATS: Foxes, feral cats and clearing of large old-growth eucalypts.

Above: Chunks of bark up to 5 cm long are stripped away from a tree's trunk, allowing the Yellow-bellied Glider access to the eucalypt sap beneath. Sap makes up most of their diet.

DIET: Sap, nectar and pollen

LENGTH: HB 27–30 cm; T 42–48 cm
WEIGHT: 450–700 g
STATUS: Near Threatened (IUCN Red List); Vulnerable (NSW); Endangered (SA)

Sugar Glider *Petaurus breviceps*

Delicate little Sugar Gliders are common around the continent's northern and eastern coasts. They are sociable possums that form groups of up to ten individuals. In the event of the untimely death of a clan member, Sugar Gliders will recruit new family members. Sugar Gliders avoid predators and conserve energy by volplaning distances of up to 50 m from tree to tree.

FEATURES: Blue-grey with cream to pale grey belly, black forehead stripe and a fluffy, often white-tipped, tail.

DIET & HABITAT: Eucalypt woodlands, rainforests and woodlands attract these small gliders, which dine on pollen, nectar, the sap of eucalypts, the gum of wattle species and some insects.

BEHAVIOUR: Sugar Gliders build a rounded nest of leaves in tree hollows, where groups may huddle together or practise torpor in cold regions. They are nocturnal and arboreal, with group members recognised by scent.

BREEDING: Season varies across range, becoming year round in the north. Two offspring stay in the pouch for 70 days, then in the nest for another 40–50 days.

THREATS: Owls, cats and competition with other mammal species (such as phascogales). Clearing of *Acacia* species.

Above: Sugar Gliders have prominent black markings on the face, including a stripe down the forehead and black behind the ears.
Opposite: Pollen, nectar and sap attract Sugar Gliders to flowering plants.

DIET: Sap, pollen, nectar and wattle seeds

LENGTH: HB 16–21 cm; T 16.5–21 cm
WEIGHT: 95–160 g
STATUS: Rare (SA); Secure elsewhere

In 1883, the Director of the Queensland Museum described the Mahogany Glider as a new species; however, it was later deemed to be the same species as the Squirrel Glider, with which it shares superficial similarities. The species was rediscovered in 1989 when an audit of the museum's specimens revealed a deceased individual that was collected near Tully in 1973. Searches in the area revealed living examples of this species, which shows distinctive differences in skull structure from the Squirrel Glider.

FEATURES: Colour may be mahogany-brown to silver-grey with a beige to apricot underside. A black dorsal stripe extends from the forehead down the spine. The tail has a dark tip and is longer than the Squirrel Glider's.

DIET & HABITAT: Prefers low-level woodlands, coastal paperbarks and grass-tree woodlands from Ingham to Tully, where it feeds on eucalypt, acacia and grass-tree sap, gum and nectar. Wattle seeds and insects are also eaten by this species.

BEHAVIOUR: This nocturnal marsupial is largely solitary and treetop-dwelling. It is rarely seen because it is a reclusive and rather silent species for a possum.

BREEDING: Birth from Apr–Oct, with one or two offspring born each season.

THREATS: Habitat destruction is a severe threat. Only an estimated 2000 remain in the wild.

Top and bottom: Cream, buff and dark mahogany colouring typify this possum, which was once confused with the Squirrel Glider. It has a longer tail and body than its relative.

DIET: Nectar, sap, gum, wattle seeds and insects

LENGTH: HB 21.5–26.5 cm; T 30–39 cm
WEIGHT: 255–410 g
STATUS: Endangered (IUCN Red List & Cmwth)

The Squirrel Glider closely resembles the smaller Sugar Glider, which overlaps its range in some areas. Both species share a similar diet and are easily mistaken, although the Squirrel Glider is larger and has a bushier tail. It is also less common than the Sugar Glider throughout most of its range.

FEATURES: Has a longer face and more pointed nose than the Sugar Glider, with longer, less rounded ears. The forehead stripe and facial markings are usually quite dark. The tail is much fluffier than the Sugar Glider's.

DIET & HABITAT: This species prefers dry sclerophyll forest and woodlands, coastal forests and wet sclerophyll forests in the north of its range. Like the Sugar Glider, it feeds on the sap of gum trees, nectar, pollen, insects and the seeds and gum of *Acacia* species.

BEHAVIOUR: Squirrel Gliders form small, gregarious groups of up to ten family members, which occupy a small home range of 20–30 ha. Families nest in a hollow, where they build a round, leaf-lined nest.

BREEDING: Similar to the Sugar Glider, and can successfully interbreed with Sugar Gliders in captivity. Breeding occurs June–Dec with two offspring produced in each litter. Maturity is reached at one year of age.

THREATS: Dingoes, cats, dogs, foxes, deforestation and land clearing.

Top to bottom: Pronounced facial markings and a bushy tail distinguish this species from the Sugar Glider; Insects are a favoured food.

DIET: Sap from wattles and eucalypts, beetles, caterpillars, wattle seeds, nectar and pollen

LENGTH: HB 18–23 cm; T 22–30 cm
WEIGHT: 190–300 g
STATUS: Vulnerable (NSW);
Threatened (Vic);
Endangered (WA)

Leadbeater's Possum was presumed extinct until 1961 when it was found living in highland Mountain Ash forest near Marysville, Victoria. Despite its common name, Leadbeater's Possum has more in common with gliders than with most other possums. Its long, prehensile tail and chisel-like incisors place it firmly in the group of other sap-suckers in the family Petauridae.

FEATURES: In appearance it is similar to the Sugar Glider, but it lacks the patagium that allows its glider relatives to soar from tree to tree. Its face is also shorter and its ears smaller. Body fur is grey to brown above and pale cream to apricot beneath. A dark dorsal stripe and black facial markings are present. The tail is long and club-shaped.

DIET & HABITAT: Dwells only in highland eucalypt forest that has a dense wattle understorey. Leadbeater's Possum feeds on insects, arthropods, plant sap and the gum of wattles.

BEHAVIOUR: Shy, swift and nocturnal, this species lives in colonies of up to eight members, which all build and share a communal nest in a hollow.

BREEDING: Births peak in May–June and Oct–Nov with one or two offspring per litter. They suckle in the pouch for up to 93 days, exiting it after 111 days.

THREATS: Juveniles are preyed on by owls. Clearing of Mountain Ash forests could be catastrophic for this species.

Top to bottom: Exudates, or gum and sap, which are licked up from tree trunks and branches, are believed to make up around 80% of this possum's diet; Mountain Ash forests are crucial habitats for Leadbeater's Possum.

DIET: Insects, arthropods, plant sap, wattle gum, honeydew and lerps

LENGTH: HB 15–17 cm; T 14.5–18 cm

WEIGHT: 100–166 g

STATUS: Endangered (IUCN Red List & Cmwth); Threatened (Vic)

The Striped Possum is unmistakable in appearance. Its black and white stripes give it a skunk-like resemblance, and, like the entirely unrelated skunk, it has also gained a bad reputation as a stinker. The Striped Possum emits a musty, pungent odour, although why it smells so strongly is not yet understood.

FEATURES: Unmistakable, with a body pattern of black and white stripes and Y-shaped facial markings. The underside of the body is white and the tail tip is usually also white. A long fourth digit on the forepaw aids in extracting wood-boring insects.

DIET & HABITAT: Striped Possums prefer rainforests and adjoining eucalypt forests on Cape York Peninsula. They are not fussy eaters, consuming foliage, fruit, small vertebrates, insects and wood-boring grubs as well as honey from native bee hives.

BEHAVIOUR: This arboreal species is swift but erratic in the canopy, where it is often heard crashing through the branches rather than seen. Its social activities are not well known, but by day it rests in a tree hollow nest.

BREEDING: Mating is probably from Feb–Aug and two young are most likely born. Males fight aggressively over females in oestrus.

THREATS: Deforestation and fire. Young may fall prey to pythons and cats.

Top and bottom: Striped Possums are extremely nimble and can execute dramatic mid-air leaps in the forest canopy. Most of the insect food is revealed by peeling off a layer of bark.

DIET: Insects, leaves, fruit and honey from native bees

LENGTH: HB 25.6–27 cm; T 31–34 cm
WEIGHT: 246–528 g
STATUS: Secure

Feathertail Glider *Acrobates pygmaeus*

The tiny Feathertail Glider is the smallest gliding mammal on Earth! It was once classified with the pygmy-possums; however, it is sufficiently different from its relatives to earn its place as Australia's only member of the family Acrobatidae. Unlike other gliders, its gliding membrane stretches only from the elbow to the knee, rather than to the ankle.

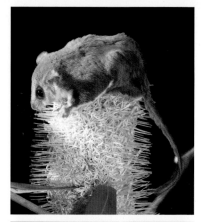

FEATURES: This is the only mammal in Australia to have a feather-like prehensile tail. Body colour is grey, with white to cream belly, and general shape appears mouse-like. A sixth pad on the sole of the hindfoot, which has an opposable first toe, also distinguishes this glider from others.

DIET & HABITAT: Prefers woodlands, rainforests and eucalypt forests along the east coast where it feeds on nectar, pollen, insects and gum tree sap.

BEHAVIOUR: Gregarious, nocturnal and arboreal, these small marsupials rest by day in dreys inside tree hollows, which they may share with up to twenty individuals.

BREEDING: Feathertail Gliders have litters of three or four young. More than one litter may be born in the late summer to winter season. Females mate soon after giving birth, and delay the embryos' development until offspring are weaned at three months.

THREATS: Kookaburras, owls, cats, foxes, dasyurids, snakes and Ghost Bats.

Top and bottom: These treetop acrobats are aided by the long feathery tail, which provides extra surface area to help the possum steer in the air. They nest and feed in small groups, often dangling by the prehensile tail.

DIET: Nectar, pollen, insects and eucalypt sap

LENGTH: HB 6.5–8 cm; T 7–8 cm
WEIGHT: 10–14 g
STATUS: Endangered (SA); Secure elsewhere

Honey Possum *Tarsipes rostratus*

The Honey Possum also holds a unique place among native mammals, being the sole member of the family Tarsipedidae and not actually a "true" possum. This marsupial original lacks claws, and instead has flat fingernails similar to those of primates. This nectarivore has a brush-tipped tongue and the fewest teeth of all marsupials.

FEATURES: The Honey Possum's protrusible tongue and sharply pointed snout are perfect for probing into flowers. Body colour is light brown to grey with three darker stripes down the back and cinnamon colour on the underside. The tapered tail is sparsely furred and prehensile.

DIET & HABITAT: Honey Possums are entirely nectarivorous, feeding on nectar and pollen in coastal heathlands through South-West Western Australia.

BEHAVIOUR: Keen olfactory senses lure the nomadic Honey Possum to pollen sources, where they often dangle upside down to get a meal. They are sociable and nocturnal, spending the day in deserted birds' nests or within hollow grass-trees where they nestle together in groups. They undergo torpor in cold weather.

BREEDING: Newborns are the smallest mammal babies and those in the same litter may have different fathers. Pouch life is two months.

THREATS: Cats and foxes are major predators. Habitat destruction.

Above: Although first recorded in 1842, the tiny Honey Possum managed to avoid scientific study until recently. Its scientific name and family classification refer to the Honey Possum's similarities to the primate Tarsier.

DIET: Feeds entirely on nectar and pollen

LENGTH: HB 4–9.4 cm; T 4.5–11 cm
WEIGHT: 7–12 g
STATUS: Secure

Common Brushtail Possum *Trichosurus vulpecula*

The Common Brushtail, like the three other brushtail species, shares a family Phalangeridae connection with the two lesser-known cuscus species and the Scaly-tailed Possum. Of them all, the Common Brushtail is the most familiar and is widely regarded as the continent's most well-known and frequently seen possum species. Its ability to exploit diverse habitats and its opportunistic feeding practices have allowed it to flourish side-by-side with humans. So prolific is it that it is considered a pest in New Zealand, where it was introduced in 1840.

FEATURES: Six recognised subspecies vary in colour from silver-grey, coppery brown in the north to shaggy black-grey in the south. A genetic mutation even produces a golden colour, but these individuals rarely survive in the wild. The prehensile tail is sometimes bushy, but always has a furless strip underneath for greater traction. The ears are long, oval-shaped and furless at the tip.

DIET & HABITAT: Common Brushtails enjoy a very large distribution, with varying populations over their range. They happily coexist with humans in suburban areas but are also found in eucalypt forests, rainforests and woodlands where they feed on leaves, fruit, flowers, insects, seeds, bird eggs and, in built-up areas, human rubbish.

BEHAVIOUR: By day, the Common Brushtail sleeps in a tree hollow, within a hollow log or wedged into a rocky crevice or ceiling. Although arboreal, they frequently come to ground to move from location to location. Individuals are solitary, occupying a home range and communicating with neighbours through scenting and guttural vocalisations.

BREEDING: Mating peaks in spring and autumn and 16–18 days afterwards a single offspring is produced, remaining in the pouch for 4–5 months. After vacating the pouch, the young possum rides its mother's back and continues to suckle for another 1–2 months.

THREATS: Dingoes, monitor lizards and pythons are native predators. Foxes, cats and dogs can also attack these possums.

DIET: Foliage, fruit, flowers, insects, bird eggs and human refuse

LENGTH: HB 35–55 cm; T 25–40 cm
WEIGHT: 1.2–4.5 kg
STATUS: Secure

Top left: A coppery coloured subspecies (*Trichosurus vulpecula johnstonii*) is found in tropical rainforests of Queensland. **Top right:** Common Brushtail possums inhabit a wide range of habitats and consume a range of food items. While fruit and leaves form the cornerstone of this species' diet, it also eats unlikely foods such as bird eggs and, on occasions, meat. **Above:** The golden colour form is caused by a rare genetic mutation and is most commonly seen in Tasmania. **Left:** Grey-brown with a creamy underbelly is one of the most commonly seen colour forms. The long, sometimes bushy prehensile tail is used to suspend the possum from branches and allow it to grasp fresh leaves, fruit or flowers.

Opposite: *Trichosurus vulpecula arnhemensis* — a Common Brushtail subspecies of tropical Northern Territory and Western Australia.

Until recently, the Short-eared Brushtail Possum and the Mountain Brushtail Possum were considered to be the same species; however, they are distinguished by the size of the ears and feet and by distribution. The Short-eared Brushtail Possum occupies subtropical rainforest and eucalypt forest along the Great Dividing Range, from South-East Qld to central NSW.

FEATURES: This possum's dark grey to black fur is flecked with white, becoming white to cream on the underside. The ears, as the name suggests, are short and rounded and the prehensile tail is black and extremely bushy, with a naked patch underneath to provide better grip.

DIET & HABITAT: This possum lives in eucalypt forests and subtropical rainforests along Australia's east coast from southern Qld to central NSW, where it feeds on foliage, flowers, fruit, seeds, lichen, bark and fungi.

BEHAVIOUR: Although they may occasionally come to ground to move from tree to tree, they are largely arboreal and nocturnal. Individuals are thought to be solitary.

BREEDING: A single offspring is produced in the breeding season from Mar–May and is usually nurtured in the pouch for four months. Maturity in females is reached at two years of age.

THREATS: Carpet Pythons, Spotted-tailed Quolls and Dingoes.

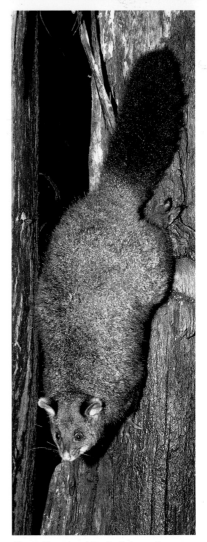

Above: Short-eared Brushtails have a long lifespan. Females live for up to seventeen years and males for up to twelve years.

DIET: Flowers, fruit, foliage, seeds, fungi, lichen and bark

LENGTH: HB 40–50 cm; T 34–42 cm
WEIGHT: 2.5–4.5 kg
STATUS: Secure

Mountain Brushtail Possum *Trichosurus cunninghami*

In 2002, genetic tests confirmed that the Mountain Brushtail Possum of the southern States was a separate species from the northern form (now the Short-eared Brushtail Possum). The species was renamed cunninghami, *after Associate Professor Ross Cunningham, who spent many years studying both species and recording their differences. Until the 1960s, the Mountain Brushtail Possum was hunted extensively for its soft pelt, which was exported to make hats for fashionable Londoners.*

FEATURES: The ears, tail and feet of the Mountain Brushtail Possum are larger than those of the Short-eared Brushtail. It is also often darker in colour, probably accounting for its colder climate, and may be grey-brown to charcoal on the upper body with a cream underside.

DIET & HABITAT: Prefers tall Mountain Ash and eucalypt forests in coastal southern New South Wales from Sydney into Victoria.

BEHAVIOUR: This species is mostly solitary and nocturnal.

BREEDING: A single offspring is produced after a 15–17 day gestation period. Strangely, when females first begin to breed they produce more males than females; however, after several years the ratio is reversed.

THREATS: Clearing of old-growth forest is a real threat for this species.

Top to bottom: A mother with a large "piggybacking" juvenile; This species was most hunted until a ban on fur exports in the 1960s.

DIET: Leaves, fruit, flowerbuds, fungi, lichen and bark

LENGTH: HB 40–50 cm; T 34–42 cm
WEIGHT: Unknown
STATUS: Secure

Scaly-tailed Possum *Wyulda squamicaudata*

This unusual species was first described in 1917 at Perth Zoo. Studies of its blood proteins show similarities to both the naked-tailed cuscuses and brushtail possums; hence, they share a family.

BEHAVIOUR: They are semi-terrestrial, solitary and nocturnal, sheltering by day in crevices in sandstone country on the Kimberley coast or in monsoon forests. Births occur during the dry season from Mar–Aug.

THREATS: Carpet Pythons and carnivorous mammals.

DIET: Flowers, fruits, foliage; possibly also consumes some insects

LENGTH: HB 31–39.5 cm; T 30 cm

WEIGHT: 1.35–2 kg

STATUS: Near Threatened (IUCN Red List); Secure nationally

Southern Common Cuscus
Phalanger intercastellanus

At first, this species was thought to be the Grey Cuscus — a Melanesian species — but it is now known as Phalanger intercastellanus, *which inhabits Australia, New Guinea and offshore islands.*

BEHAVIOUR: Climbs slowly and carefully in the treetops, but bounds when infrequently seen on the ground. It is nocturnal and solitary within its tropical rainforest environment.

THREATS: Scrub Pythons and Carpet Pythons.

DIET: Fruit, flowers, flowerbuds, leaves; possibly also eats insects and small birds and their eggs

LENGTH: HB 35– 40 cm; T 28–35 cm

WEIGHT: 1.5–2.2 kg

STATUS: Rare (Qld)

Common Spotted Cuscus *Spilocuscus maculatus*

The Common Spotted Cuscus was discovered a full 90 years before its more secretive cousin the Southern Common Cuscus. It is thought that tales of monkeys in the northern forests of Cape York originated from fleeting glimpses of this species' bare face and bugged eyes peering down from rainforest canopy.

FEATURES: Silver-grey, woolly fur is darker around the top of the face, which is bare and pink, as are the paws. White, pale or chestnut blotches on the body give it a spotted appearance. Bare, rasp-like skin increases traction on the underside of the tail, which terminates in a furless tip.

DIET & HABITAT: Inhabits open eucalypt forests and mangrove forests, but prefers tropical rainforests where it feeds on fruit, foliage, flowers and insects. In captivity, they have been known to eat some meat and eggs, and most likely do so in the wild.

BEHAVIOUR: Cuscuses are slow-moving and solitary with a low metabolic rate. They are mostly nocturnal and sleep by day. In hot weather they pant. Males are aggressive with other males.

BREEDING: The Common Spotted Cuscus may be able to breed all year, but little is known about this aspect of its lifestyle. Females probably give birth to two to four offspring, with only one surviving to adulthood.

THREATS: Scrub Pythons.

Above: Having a tail that is prehensile, strong and naked on the underside means slow-moving Common Spotted Cuscuses can use this appendage as a fifth limb to pull themselves through the rainforest canopy.

DIET: Fruit, leaves, flowers, insects; possibly some birds and their eggs and nestlings

LENGTH: HB 34.8–58 cm; T 31–43.5 cm
WEIGHT: 1.5–4.9 kg
STATUS: Rare (Qld)

Living with Macropods

In Greek, the term *macropod* literally means "big foot" — an apt name for this group of mammals. One notable macropod, the kangaroo, features on Australia's coat-of-arms and serves as a mascot for many sporting teams. Most Australians have come face-to-face with these macropods at some point, either at fauna and wildlife parks or in their own backyards. So common are macropods that it is not unusual for Australians to have a "pet" joey that they are raising until it is old enough to return to the wild.

Potoroids

The group of small macropod marsupials known as potoroids includes the omnivorous potoroos and their bettong and rat-kangaroo kin. All of them retain some of the features of their ancient mammalian ancestors, with weakly prehensile tails used to gather nesting materials. Australia has three potoroo species, five living bettong species and one rat-kangaroo. Only one, the Rufous Bettong, has escaped the ill-effects of human occupation — all others have declined in population. A fascinating relative, the sole member of the subfamily Hypsiprymnodontinae, is the Musky Rat-kangaroo. This small marsupial is believed to be the most primitive of macropods, with a likely ancestry from possum-like creatures. It is the only species that commonly gives birth to twins.

Rufous Bettong *Aepyprymnus rufescens*

The Rufous Bettong is Australia's most widely distributed potoroid species. It is another of the nest-builders, excavating shallow depressions over which it constructs dome-shaped nests of fibrous plant material.

BEHAVIOUR: Rufous Bettongs are nocturnal and form small groups. Up to five nests are used sporadically across this bettong's 45–110 ha home range.

THREATS: Dingoes, feral cats and dogs.

DIET: Grass, herbs, roots, tubers, flowers, carrion

LENGTH: HB 37.5–39 cm; T 33.8–38.7 cm

WEIGHT: 3–3.5 kg

STATUS: Vulnerable (NSW); Threatened (Vic); Secure elsewhere.

Southern Bettong *Bettongia gaimardi*

This species probably became locally extinct on the Australian mainland sometime in the early 20th century. It is also known as the Tasmanian or Eastern Bettong.

BEHAVIOUR: Strictly nocturnal and mostly solitary. During the day, they rest in a nest of bark and grass. Births are recorded year round with a single joey born after a gestation period of 21 days.

THREATS: Habitat clearing, feral cats and dogs.

DIET: Underground fungi, roots, bulbs, seeds

LENGTH: HB 31.5–33.2 cm; T 28.8–34.5 cm

WEIGHT: 1.2–2.25 kg

STATUS: Near Threatened (IUCN Red List); Extinct (NSW); Threatened (Tas)

Burrowing Bettong *Bettongia lesueur*

Burrowing Bettongs are now locally extinct on the mainland and exist only on Bernier, Dorre, Barrow and Boodie Islands off the central coast of WA.

BEHAVIOUR: The only truly burrowing macropod — up to 100 individuals share a series of complex burrows or warrens. Burrowing Bettongs are very vocal, making squeaks, squeals, grunts and hisses.

THREATS: Foxes and feral cats impact severely on this species.

DIET: Fungi, tubers, roots, invertebrates, flowers, seeds and carrion

LENGTH: HB 28–36 cm; T 21.5–30 cm

WEIGHT: c. 1.5 kg

STATUS: Vulnerable (IUCN Red List)

Brush-tailed Bettong *Bettongia penicillata*

The Brush-tailed Bettong — or Woylie as it is also known — is easily distinguished by the "brush" of dark hair on its tail.

BEHAVIOUR: The Brush-tailed Bettong is nocturnal and solitary, although it shares overlapping home ranges. The species is easily identified by its peculiar zig-zagging hop. This bettong shelters in a domed nest by day.

THREATS: Foxes and habitat destruction.

DIET: Fungi, tubers, roots and small arthropods

LENGTH: HB 30–38 cm; T 29–36 cm

WEIGHT: 1.1–1.6 kg

STATUS: Conservation Dependent (IUCN Red List; Threatened (Vic); Rare (SA); Extinct (NT)

Northern Bettong *Bettongia tropica*

Similar to the Brush-tailed Bettong, of which it was once considered a subspecies. Populations are confined to just three areas in Qld's north.

BEHAVIOUR: Strictly nocturnal and largely solitary. Rests in a nest by day. Females are able to breed year round, and may have three joeys a year when environmental conditions are favourable.

THREATS: Fire affects the availability of underground fruiting bodies of fungi — a major element of this species' diet.

DIET: Fungi, roots, tubers, limited seeds and insects

LENGTH: HB 26.7–40.4 cm; T 31.7–36.4 cm

WEIGHT: 900–1400 g

STATUS: Endangered (IUCN Red List & Cmwth); Extinct (NSW)

Gilbert's Potoroo *Potorous gilbertii*

Gilbert's Potoroo is Australia's most critically endangered mammalian species. Only an estimated 40 individuals are believed to survive in the wild at Two Peoples Bay Nature Reserve, WA.

BEHAVIOUR: Nocturnal, with each animal occupying an overlapping home range. Hops using the hindlimbs only, but may use the forepaws for balance when walking and foraging.

THREATS: Burning of shrubland; cats, foxes and Dingoes.

DIET: Heavily reliant on the fruiting bodies of underground fungi

LENGTH: HB 27 cm; T 21 cm

WEIGHT: 900–1200 g

STATUS: Critically Endangered (IUCN Red List)

Long-footed Potoroo *Potorous longipes*

The Long-footed Potoroo has longer hindfeet and a longer tail than the very similar-looking Long-nosed Potoroo. It also has a leathery hallucal pad on the sole of its foot, which is absent in its relative.

BEHAVIOUR: The Long-footed Potoroo is nocturnal, sheltering by day. It moves with short, bipedal hops and may vocalise with a quiet "kiss kiss" sound.

THREATS: Dingoes, foxes, feral dogs, cats, logging and land clearing.

DIET: Largely reliant on underground and sub-underground fungi

LENGTH: HB 38–41.5 cm; T 31.5–32.5 cm

WEIGHT: 1.6–2.2 kg

STATUS: Endangered (IUCN Red List & Cmwth)

Long-nosed Potoroo *Potorous tridactylus*

This species was one of Australia's first recorded small mammals, with an illustration and description given in 1789 by Governor Arthur Phillip at Botany Bay.

BEHAVIOUR: Nocturnal and mostly solitary, but sometimes feeds in small parties. Breeds mostly in winter and spring and usually produces two offspring each year. Slightly less dependent on a fungal diet than the Long-footed Potoroo.

THREATS: Dingoes, dogs, cats, owls, foxes and land clearing.

DIET: Fungi, roots, tubers, insects, soft-bodied invertebrates

LENGTH: HB 34–38 cm; T 19.8–26.2 cm

WEIGHT: 660–1640 g

STATUS: Vulnerable (Cmwth); Threatened (Vic)

Musky Rat-kangaroo *Hypsiprymnodon moschatus*

Australia's smallest macropod is only loosely related to other potoroid species, being the sole living member of the subfamily Hypsiprymnodontidae.

BEHAVIOUR: Diurnal and crepuscular. They are terrestrial, but an opposable "big toe" on the hindfeet enables them to leap over and climb through fallen trees. Another unusual feature is this species' bounding, quadrupedal gait.

THREATS: Clearing of land for agriculture and fragmentation of rainforest are a concern for this species.

DIET: Fruit, insects, fungi and seeds

LENGTH: HB 15.3–27.3 cm; T 12.3–15.9 cm

WEIGHT: 360–680 g

STATUS: Secure

Spectacled Hare-wallaby *Lagorchestes conspicillatus*

This stocky, thick-set, greyish-brown macropod is one of the most easily identifiable thanks to the "spectacles" of reddish fur around the eyes.

BEHAVIOUR: Nocturnal, resting in tunnels in grassland by day. They are solitary but sometimes feed in groups of three, moving with a bouncy, bipedal hop. Danger is communicated by a low warning hiss.

THREATS: Competition with graziers. Predation by feral cats.

DIET: Green tips of grasses, shrubs and herbs

LENGTH: HB 40–47 cm; T 37–49 cm

WEIGHT: 1.6–4.5 kg

STATUS: Near Threatened (IUCN Red List & NT)

Rufous Hare-wallaby *Lagorchestes hirsutus*

Commonly known as the Mala, this species features in the Dreaming stories of the Anangu people of Uluru–Kata Tjuta National Park, where a captive population has been re-introduced to a feral-proof enclosure.

BEHAVIOUR: They are solitary, nocturnal and terrestrial, preferring a habitat where they hide in spinifex grasslands and coastal shrub.

THREATS: Feral cats and human inhabitation impact on this species, which, in the wild, is confined to Bernier and Dorre Islands off WA.

DIET: Green shoots and tips of grasses, shrubs and herbs, some insects

LENGTH: HB 31–39 cm; T 24.5–30.5 cm

WEIGHT: 780–1960 g

STATUS: Vulnerable (IUCN Red List)

Banded Hare-wallaby *Lagostrophus fasciatus*

This species' banded rump distinguishes it from other hare-wallaby species, but it is only distantly related to the Lagorchestes *species and is thought to descend from the ancient sthenurine kangaroos.*

BEHAVIOUR: Solitary within a home range that, for males, overlaps female territory. Males are aggressive with other males. In tough times, embryonic diapause is enlisted as a reproductive strategy.

THREATS: Feral cats, habitat destruction and slow reproductive rate.

DIET: Shrubs, spinifex grasses, legumes and dicotyledonous plants

LENGTH: HB 40–50 cm; T 35–40 cm

WEIGHT: 1.5–3 kg

STATUS: Vulnerable (IUCN Red List)

Tasmanian Pademelon *Thylogale billardierii*

Having fallen victim to the 19th-century fur and leather trade on the mainland, this species now exists only in Tasmania and the larger islands of Bass Strait.

BEHAVIOUR: Nocturnal, shy and reluctant to venture too far out of densely vegetated rainforest or wet sclerophyll forest. Rarely vocal, but bucks may give the odd guttural hiss of aggression or make clucking sounds when courting.

THREATS: Habitat destruction. It has few predators in Tasmania.

DIET: Insects and other arthropods, small lizards
LENGTH: HB 56–63 cm; T 32–48.3 cm
WEIGHT: 2.4–12 kg
STATUS: Secure (Tas)

Red-legged Pademelon *Thylogale stigmatica*

Widely distributed, this species is distinguished from its Red-necked relative by its fur, which has more of a rufous tinge — particularly on the legs.

BEHAVIOUR: Diurnal, but adopts a slumped resting position against a trunk during midday heat. These pademelons are highly vocal, with males making a clucking that is met with harsh rasping from uninterested females.

THREATS: Dingoes, Spotted-tailed Quolls and Scrub Pythons.

DIET: Rainforest fruit, grasses, herbs and ferns
LENGTH: HB 38.6–53.6 cm; T 30.1–47.3 cm
WEIGHT: 2.5–6.8 kg
STATUS: Vulnerable (NSW); Secure elsewhere

Red-necked Pademelon *Thylogale thetis*

Red-necked Pademelons are charcterised by a rufous patch on the neck and the way the tail is held stiffly straight out behind when they hop.

BEHAVIOUR: The stiff tail also prevents them from using pentapedal locomotion and they forage on all fours but hop bipedally. They move to feeding grounds through "tunnels" of vegetation. Foot thumps and growls are used to communicate when feeding in groups.

THREATS: Dogs, Dingoes, foxes, large birds of prey and land clearing.

DIET: Grass and shrubs
LENGTH: HB 29–62 cm; T 27–51 cm
WEIGHT: 1.8–9.1 kg
STATUS: Secure

Larger Macropods

Large macropods (wallabies, wallaroos and kangaroos) in the genus *Macropus* occupy most of the Australian continent. Among their relatives are the true originals of the macropod world — animals such as the Quokka, Swamp Wallaby and the two tree-kangaroos. All of these unique macropods have evolved specialist lifestyles and features that set them apart from their relatives. Also rendered different — largely by habitat and many decades of existing in isolated pockets of land — are the many closely related rock-wallabies. Rock-wallabies occupy a chain of relic habitat in rocky terrain. Over time, species become separated from others of their kind, creating many similar-looking but genetically distinct populations.

Agile Wallaby *Macropus agilis*

A prominent white stripe on the thigh is a typical indicator of this species, which is widespread throughout Australia's tropical north and in New Guinea.

BEHAVIOUR: Agile Wallabies form mobs of up to ten, which are dominated by a single buck. Foot thumping alerts others to danger. Females breed year round and exhibit embryonic diapause.

THREATS: Dingoes, Wedge-tailed Eagles, feral cats and foxes.

DIET: Grass and some roots
LENGTH:
HB 59.3–85 cm;
T 58.7–84 cm
WEIGHT: 9–27 kg
STATUS: Secure

Black-striped Wallaby *Macropus dorsalis*

The black stripe running down this species' forehead is its defining feature and the reason for its common name. This macropod's nose, digits and ear tips are also black.

BEHAVIOUR: Forms mobs of twenty that move along runways in vegetation to feeding grounds. Females mature before males, can mate immediately after giving birth and use embryonic diapause.

THREATS: Dingoes, Wedge-tailed Eagles and competition from stock.

DIET: Grass and leaves
LENGTH: HB 53–82 cm;
T 54–83 cm
WEIGHT: 6–20 kg
STATUS: Endangered (NSW); Secure elsewhere

Tammar Wallaby *Macropus eugenii*

Only small populations of this shaggy little wallaby exist on the mainland. Its main haunts are islands off the coast of WA and SA where, amazingly, this species is known to drink seawater.

BEHAVIOUR: Nocturnal and solitary, but may feed in small groups after dark. They graze on grassy clearings close to runways in denser cover.

THREATS: Seasonal starvation, feral cats and land clearing.

DIET: Mostly dry grasses
LENGTH: HB 52–68 cm; T 33–45 cm
WEIGHT: 4–10 kg
STATUS: Near Threatened (IUCN Red List); Secure nationally

Western Brush Wallaby *Macropus irma*

This wallaby's black-tipped paws are the reason for its other common name, Black-gloved Wallaby. It prefers open woodlands with seasonal fresh pick.

BEHAVIOUR: Western Brush Wallabies are solitary and diurnal, becoming active in the early morning and late afternoon and spending the hotter parts of the day in the shade of bushes or thickets.

THREATS: Foxes are major predators. Habitat clearing could affect this species.

DIET: Grass, particularly fresh shoots
LENGTH: HB 90–120 cm; T 54–97 cm
WEIGHT: 7–9 kg
STATUS: Near Threatened (IUCN Red List)

Parma Wallaby *Macropus parma*

Although presumed extinct by the mid 1960s, this small wallaby was re-discovered in New Zealand and repatriated. In 1967, a small group of local individuals was also discovered, reversing this species' extinct status.

BEHAVIOUR: Nocturnal and solitary but sometimes feed in pairs. They live in dense, shrubby understoreys. Females mature at one year of age.

THREATS: Dingoes, feral cats, Wedge-tailed Eagles and land clearing.

DIET: Grass, herbs, ferns
LENGTH: HB 44.7–52.8 cm; T 40.5–54.4 cm
WEIGHT: 3.2–5.9 kg
STATUS: Vulnerable (NSW); Near Threatened (IUCN Red List)

Whiptail Wallaby *Macropus parryi*

Dainty and distinctively marked, this wallaby is sometimes also known as the Pretty-face Wallaby. It is arid-adapted and rarely needs to drink except during times of drought.

BEHAVIOUR: This is a diurnal and sociable species that forms large mobs of up to 50 individuals that operate under the social hierarchy of the dominant bucks.

THREATS: Predation by raptors and feral cats. Habitat destruction.

DIET: Grass, herbs and ferns
LENGTH: HB 61–92.4 cm; T 72.8–104.5 cm
WEIGHT: 7–26 kg
STATUS: Secure

Red-necked Wallaby *Macropus rufogriseus*

Forest, woodlands and coastal heath are this species' preferred environments. A Tasmanian subspecies of the Red-necked Wallaby is locally known as Bennett's Wallaby.

BEHAVIOUR: Groups of 30 form to feed on abundantly grassed areas, but this species is mostly solitary and nocturnal. Females breed year round.

THREATS: Feral cats and Dingoes on the mainland. Habitat destruction.

DIET: Grass, herbs and some seeds
LENGTH: HB 65.9–92.3 cm; T 62.3–79 cm
WEIGHT: 11–26.8 kg
STATUS: Rare (SA); Secure elsewhere

Bridled Nailtail Wallaby *Onychogalea fraenata*

Nailtail wallabies have a peculiar hard, pointed "nail" at the end of the tail, which gives them their name. This species was considered extinct until 1973 when it was found on farmland that is now the Taunton Scientific Reserve.

BEHAVIOUR: Diurnal and does not form colonies. Its habit of hiding rather than running when threatened has led to its decline.

THREATS: Competition with stock. Dingoes, foxes and feral cats.

DIET: Forbs, chenopods and soft-leaved grasses
LENGTH: HB 43–70 cm; T 36–54 cm
WEIGHT: 4–8 kg
STATUS: Endangered (IUCN Red List & Cmwth)

Allied Rock-wallaby *Petrogale assimilis*

Lacking prominent markings, this species can be difficult to distinguish from other similar rock-wallabies. It was first discovered on Palm Island and recorded to science in 1877.

BEHAVIOUR: Mostly nocturnal. Forms colonies based on hierarchy of age, in which males and females form pairs and mutually groom.

THREATS: Dingoes, foxes and Wedge-tailed Eagles. Land clearing.

DIET: Forbs, shrubs, fruit, seeds and flowers
LENGTH: HB 44.5–59 cm; T 40.9–55 cm
WEIGHT: 4.3–4.7 kg
STATUS: Secure

Short-eared Rock-wallaby *Petrogale brachyotis*

Although this species is quite common across its Arnhem Land range, it is one of the continent's least-studied rock-wallabies, owing largely to its isolation.

BEHAVIOUR: Short-eared Rock-wallabies are nocturnal, but are often seen by day basking on hot rocks in their craggy habitat. They form colonies and are adept hoppers, nimbly bounding off if alarmed.

THREATS: Dingoes are frequent predators of juveniles. Land clearing.

DIET: Grass, sedges and seeds
LENGTH: HB 40.5–55 cm; T 32–55 cm
WEIGHT: 3.5–5.6 kg
STATUS: Secure

Monjon *Petrogale burbidgei*

The Monjon, or Warabi as it is often known, is Australia's smallest rock-wallaby and was only discovered in 1978 (in part because of its similarities to the Nabarlek). It occupies open woodland in high-rainfall areas of the Kimberley, WA.

BEHAVIOUR: By day, Monjons rests in rock crevices, caves or under overhangs. They are sociable and swift, vanishing quickly if disturbed.

THREATS: Dingoes, feral cats, White-bellied Sea-Eagles, drought and fire.

DIET: Grass, leaves and fruit
LENGTH: HB 30.6–35.3 cm; T 26.4–29 cm
WEIGHT: 960–1430 g
STATUS: Near Threatened (IUCN Red List)

Nabarlek *Petrogale concinna*

The second-smallest of Australia's rock-wallaby species, the Nabarlek has unique teeth — it is equipped with an unlimited supply of supernumerary molars. As its teeth grind down, more molars erupt at the back of the jaw and move forward to replace worn-out teeth.

BEHAVIOUR: Timid and nocturnal but may bask on hot rocks by day.

THREATS: White-bellied Sea-Eagles. Dry season fires kill many Nabarleks.

DIET: Ferns, sedges and grass

LENGTH: HB 29–35 cm; T 22–31 cm

WEIGHT: 1–1.7 kg

STATUS: Near Threatened (IUCN Red List & NT)

Black-footed Rock-wallaby *Petrogale lateralis*

This species includes three recognised subspecies — Petrogale lateralis lateralis, P. l. hacketti *and* P. l. pearsoni *— as well as two races in the west Kimberley and MacDonnell Ranges.*

BEHAVIOUR: Naturalist John Gilbert wrote in the 1840s that this was a "remarkably shy and wary animal". Although nocturnal, colonies of this wallaby may be seen basking by day.

THREATS: Red Foxes are predators.

DIET: Grass, leaves and some fruit

LENGTH: (*P. l. lateralis*) HB 44.6–52.9 cm; T 40.7–60.5 cm

WEIGHT: 3.1–5 kg

STATUS: Subspecies are Vulnerable in parts

Mareeba Rock-wallaby *Petrogale mareeba*

Granted species status as late as 1992, this wallaby is superficially very similar to the Sharman's and Allied Rock-wallabies and almost impossible to tell apart from them without genetic testing.

BEHAVIOUR: Forms colonies of up to 100 individuals. Nocturnal, resting in caves or under overhangs by day. Males and females form lasting pairs and mutually groom.

THREATS: Dingoes, foxes and clearing of land between rocky patches.

DIET: Grass, shrubs and leaves

LENGTH: HB 42.5–54.8 cm; T 41.5–53 cm

WEIGHT: 3.8–4.5 kg

STATUS: Rare (Qld)

Brush-tailed Rock-wallaby *Petrogale penicillata*

The Brush-tailed Rock-wallaby was heavily targeted by the 19th-century fur trade. It was Australia's first classified rock-wallaby, being named Kangurus penicillatus *in 1825 and later gaining its current scientific name.*

BEHAVIOUR: Nimble and nocturnal, but may be seen basking by day. Forms small, sociable colonies.

THREATS: Dingoes and foxes. Competes with rabbits, stock and feral goats.

DIET: Grass, forbs, seeds, fruit and flowers

LENGTH:
HB 51–58.6 cm;
T 50–70 cm

WEIGHT: 4.7–10.9 kg

STATUS: Vulnerable (IUCN Red List & Cmwth)

Proserpine Rock-wallaby *Petrogale persephone*

Despite its range being situated quite close to a populated area, this large rock-wallaby species was overlooked until 1976.

BEHAVIOUR: Sometimes leaps up sloping trees, but is not arboreal. Partly diurnal and may be seen basking by day. Males may be more than twice the size of females. Prefers areas with a grassy understorey.

THREATS: Limited range, so very susceptible to habitat destruction.

DIET: Grass, broad-leaved plants, pandanus and coastal shrubs

LENGTH: HB 52.6–63 cm;
T 51.5–67.5 cm

WEIGHT: 3.5–9.5 kg

STATUS: Endangered (IUCN Red List & Cmwth)

Yellow-footed Rock-wallaby
Petrogale xanthopus

The attractive coat of this species — the largest rock-wallaby — made the Yellow-footed Rock-wallaby popular quarry for the fur trade and it was heavily exploited in the 19th century. Its long, banded tail is its most distinctive feature.

BEHAVIOUR: Forms colonies of up to 100 rock-wallabies, each with an overlapping home range of up to 200 ha. Both sexes mature at two years.

THREATS: Dingoes, Wedge-tailed Eagles and competition with stock.

DIET: Grass, forbs and foliage

LENGTH: HB 48–65 cm;
T 56.5–70 cm

WEIGHT: 6–12 kg

STATUS: Near Threatened (IUCN Red List); Endangered (NSW); Vulnerable (SA)

Bennett's Tree-kangaroo *Dendrolagus bennettianus*

Unusually, Australia's two tree-kangaroo species are the only macropods to have returned to their ancestors' arboreal lifestyles. The rainforest-dwelling Bennett's Tree-kangaroo is the larger of the two.

BEHAVIOUR: These wary animals defend a small home territory in the treetops, where they move with dexterity despite lacking a prehensile tail. Males' ranges overlap those of several females.

THREATS: Dingoes, Scrub Pythons and deforestation.

DIET: Foliage, leaves and fruit of rainforest plant species

LENGTH: HB 69–75 cm; T 73–84 cm

WEIGHT: 8–13.7 kg

STATUS: Near Threatened (IUCN Red List); Rare (Qld)

Lumholtz's Tree-kangaroo
Dendrolagus lumholtzi

Aborigines of the Atherton Tableland and Herbert River knew this species as Boongarry, Mabi or Muppie for many years before it was brought to scientific attention in 1882.

BEHAVIOUR: Sleeps by day slumped in a tree fork and is active by night. Mostly solitary but may feed in groups. Wooing males are aggressive with other males but cluck and paw at females.

THREATS: Deforestation, owls, pythons and feral cats.

DIET: Fruit and foliage including Ribbonwood and Wild Tobacco leaves

LENGTH: HB 52–65 cm; T 65.5–73.6 cm

WEIGHT: 5.1–8.6 kg

STATUS: Near Threatened (IUCN Red List); Rare (Qld)

Quokka *Setonix brachyurus*

The unique Quokka differs from all other macropods in dentition, chromosomal composition, skull structure and blood proteins. Navigator Willem de Vlamingh first recorded it on Rottnest Island in 1696.

BEHAVIOUR: Gregarious and diurnal, Quokkas form hierarchical colonies that congregate around freshwater soaks or heavily vegetated swamps.

THREATS: Foxes on the mainland and dehydration.

DIET: Grass, leaves, sedges and succulent plants, which are low in nutrients on Rottnest Island

LENGTH: HB 40–54 cm; T 24.5–31 cm

WEIGHT: 2.7–4.2 kg

STATUS: Vulnerable (IUCN Red List & Cmwth)

Swamp Wallaby *Wallabia bicolor*

The sole member of the genus **Wallabia**, this macropod could be said to be the only true wallaby. It has fewer chromosomes than other wallabies and prefers browsing to grazing. It also has a distinctive, low-bodied hopping gait.

BEHAVIOUR: Swamp Wallabies are more diurnal than most wallaby species, foraging or resting by day. Although mostly solitary, they feed in groups at night.

THREATS: Dingoes, feral cats and Wedge-tailed Eagles.

DIET: Shrubs, ferns and grass across a range of habitats

LENGTH: HB 66.5–84.7 cm; T 64–86 cm

WEIGHT: 10.3–20.5 kg

STATUS: Vulnerable (SA); Secure elsewhere

Antilopine Wallaroo *Macropus antilopinus*

Slender and kangaroo-like, this wallaroo is probably often confused with the Red Kangaroo or grey kangaroos, but it is distinguished from these by its white-tipped ears.

DIET: Feeds almost entirely on grass

LENGTH: HB 77.8–120 cm; T 67.9–89 cm

WEIGHT: 16–49 kg

STATUS: Secure

BEHAVIOUR: This gregarious species lives in mobs of 8–30 individuals, with larger mobs found when food is plentiful. They are mostly nocturnal but may become more diurnal during the wet season.

THREATS: Dingoes, eagles and sometimes sea-eagles.

Black Wallaroo *Macropus bernardus*

Australia's smallest and shyest wallaroo, the Black Wallaroo is easily identified by its colour and its stocky shape. It has chromosomal differences to the other wallaroos and exists only in a limited NT range.

DIET: Grass, shrubs and ground plants

LENGTH: HB 59.5–72.5 cm; T 54.5–64 cm

WEIGHT: 13–22 kg

STATUS: Near Threatened (IUCN Red List)

BEHAVIOUR: Solitary, shy and seldom seen in groups of more than a female and joey with one male. Black Wallaroos feed in the evening but may be seen by day during the wet season.

THREATS: Dingoes, drought and bushfire.

Common Wallaroo *Macropus robustus*

This solid, long-eared wallaroo species was first recorded in drawings made by Joseph Banks in 1770, when the Endeavour *was being repaired at the Endeavour River in north Queensland. In its western range, the subspecies* erubescens *is commonly known as the Euro.*

FEATURES: Dark grey-brown fur often with a rufous tinge on the flank and back. Females with blue-grey or brown body fur. Underparts are pale grey to silver, as are the forelimbs and hindlimbs, although the paws and toes are reddish black. The nose is black and the ears are exceptionally large and flared.

DIET & HABITAT: Widely distributed over the mainland in varied habitats but mostly rocky terrain, hills and escarpments. This species can survive with very little water, provided it can shelter from the sun and consume succulent plants. Its preferred diet is grass, shrubs and succulent plants.

BEHAVIOUR: Nocturnal and solitary. Will emit a loud hiss as it exhales if alarmed. Another common vocalisation is a loud "cch-cch" noise.

BREEDING: Offspring are produced year round, but breeding may cease during drought. Gestation time differs for the *erubescens* (Euro) subspecies.

THREATS: Domestic livestock may compete with this species. Dingoes and Wedge-tailed Eagles are its main predators.

Top and bottom: Large ears, black paws and nose, and a distinctive stance typify this species.

DIET: Grass, ground plants and shrubs

LENGTH: HB 110.7–198.6 cm; T 53.4–90.1 cm
WEIGHT: 6.25–46.5 kg
STATUS: Secure

Western Grey Kangaroo *Macropus fuliginosus*

At one time there were thought to be as many as five grey kangaroo species. Biologists have now confirmed that there are just two species, which are distinguished largely by reproductive behaviour. Female Western Grey Kangaroos, unlike their similar Eastern Grey relatives, do not exhibit embryonic diapause and have shorter oestrous and gestation periods.

FEATURES: Superficially similar to Eastern Greys, but usually darker brown in colour on the face and upper body with a thicker coat. The underparts are a pale fawn to buff brown. The tips of the hindpaws and forepaws are darker brown to black, as is the tail tip. Males, sometimes known colloquially as "stinkers", emit a pungent body odour.

DIET & HABITAT: Populations spread throughout southern WA, SA, western Vic, north-western NSW and south-western Qld. A subspecies is found on Kangaroo Island, SA. They prefer flat plains and open woodland with a grassy understorey and feed on grass, broad-leaved plants and some shrubs.

BEHAVIOUR: Crepuscular and gregarious, forming large mobs led by a dominant buck.

BREEDING: After a gestation period averaging 30.5 days, a single joey is born and remains in the pouch for about 42 weeks, which is about fourteen weeks less than the pouch life of the Eastern Grey. The female Western Grey's oestrous cycle is also shorter, averaging just 35 days.

THREATS: Dingoes, cats, Wedge-tailed Eagles and habitat destruction.

Above: A Western Grey examines a twig for any signs of sustenance. Western Greys have darker, fluffier fur than their Eastern Grey relatives.

DIET: Grass, ground plants, shrubs and crops (when available)

LENGTH: HB 52.1–122.5 cm; T 42.5–100 cm
WEIGHT: 3–53.5 kg
STATUS: Secure

Eastern Grey Kangaroo *Macropus giganteus*

Coastal plains along Australia's eastern seaboard in Qld, NSW, Vic, Tas and the south-eastern corner of SA are the preferred environments of the Eastern Grey. They are abundant within this range. Eastern Greys are slightly paler than Western Greys, with which they share a small part of their range.

FEATURES: Slightly less fluffy than Western Greys, these "roos" are usually a grey-brown to silver-grey colour above, with pale, light grey underparts. The tips of the forepaws and hindfeet are darker brown, as is the tip of the tail. The large, oblong ears are often fringed with white hairs in the inner corners.

DIET & HABITAT: Inhabits coastal woodlands, plains, the undulating landscape of the Great Dividing Range and eastern coast areas with rainfall greater than 250 mm per annum. Also recorded in mallee scrub and tea-tree woodlands. Frequently visits farmlands.

BEHAVIOUR: Crepuscular and sociable, congregating in large mobs of up to 100 individuals. Males and females within the mob have separate hierarchies based on age and reproductive standing. They make a number of vocalisations. Males wooing a female in oestrus mimic soft maternal clucks. If alarmed, they make a guttural coughing noise.

BREEDING: Gestation takes about 36 days and births occur year round, peaking in summer. Twins are rarely produced, but have been recorded. Usually a single joey is born and vacates the pouch eleven months later.

THREATS: Dingoes, cats, eagles and habitat destruction.

Above: Joeys remain in the pouch for around eleven months. Like many kangaroo and wallaby species, females can practise embryonic diapause when conditions are not favourable.

DIET: Grasses, forbs and leaves

LENGTH: HB 54.2–121.2 cm; T 43–109 cm

WEIGHT: 3.5–66 kg

STATUS: Rare (SA); Secure elsewhere

Red Kangaroo *Macropus rufus*

At over 1.4 m tall, the adult male Red Kangaroo is the largest marsupial on the planet. It is also the only kangaroo that is truly suited to arid environments; however, it prefers the greener plains and open woodlands where there are plenty of green herbaceous plants to forage on.

FEATURES: Males, or "boomers", are heavily muscled with a rich, rusty red coat, although some may also be a dark grey. Females, often called "blue-flyers", are much smaller and are grey-blue to reddish. Colours vary with location and season. A broader snout and white cheek stripe, extending to beneath the ears, along with their larger size, distinguishes Red Kangaroos from Eastern and Western Greys.

DIET & HABITAT: Grasslands and woodlands in arid, semi-arid or more well-watered regions. Their preferred diet is fresh green grass, native herbs and the foliage of some shrubs.

BEHAVIOUR: These are mob animals, forming small groups. When food is plentiful, hundreds may gather to feed. They are largely crepuscular, feeding at dawn and dusk and resting in the shade during the day. Body heat is regulated in hot weather by panting and licking the forearms.

BREEDING: Females exhibit embryonic diapause, which may allow them to have three joeys, all in different stages of development, at any one time — a quiescent blastocyst, a joey in the pouch (drinking from one teat) and a joey at foot (suckling from another teat). Remarkably, the composition of the milk differs for pouch young and young at heel, which drink from a different teat.

THREATS: Dingoes and Wedge-tailed Eagles. Annual quotas are set for professional, licensed shooters, but this sustainable culling for the commercial kangaroo industry appears to have little impact on populations.

Above: This joey has almost reached "eviction" stage. **Opposite, top to bottom:** Boomers are the hierarchical leaders of the pack; Females are much greyer in colour than males.

DIET: Grass, forbs and crops (when available)

LENGTH: HB 74.5–140 cm; T 64.5–100 cm
WEIGHT: 17–85 kg
STATUS: Secure

Placental Mammals

Placental mammals, or eutherian mammals, are those with which we — as primate placental mammals — probably most readily identify (however, our relationship with the rodents has often been less than friendly).

Placental mammals are more diverse and widespread than any other mammal group. They include the sea mammals, such as whales and dolphins (which are featured in a separate Steve Parish Wild Australia Guide), flying mammals such as bats and flying-foxes, and common terrestrial domestic animals such as dogs, cats, cows and horses.

Bats are the only mammals that are truly able to fly, and were the first placental mammals to colonise Australia, arriving approximately 55 million years ago according to the fossil record. Today, the honour of being the largest and most successful order among Australia's native placental mammals must go to the rodents, many of which are rarely seen or may be mistaken for introduced "vermin".

Of the larger eutherian mammals in the order Carnivora, Australia has just one species — the Dingo — which is considered native but is actually related to the Indian Wolf and first appeared in Australia about 3000 years ago.

Above: Australia's wild dog species may have been introduced by Aborigines or Asian fishermen, but many believe them to be a subspecies of wolf.
Right: Australia's native rodents are plentiful but little studied. **Opposite:** Bats were the first to take advantage of Australia's lack of placental mammal competition.

Bats

Bats are specialised flying mammals that may have evolved from a primitive gliding mammal, such as a shrew. They all have thin membranous wings and keeled sternums where the muscles necessary for flight are attached. Bats can be divided into two groups — megabats and microbats. Megabats, in the suborder Megachiroptera, are larger, are mostly fructivores and use their keen eyesight to navigate. Microbats (suborder Microchiroptera) are generally much smaller, insectivorous and use bisonar echolocation to find their way around in the dark.

Black Flying-fox *Pteropus alecto*

With a wingspan of more than 1 m, this is one of the largest bat species on Earth. It inhabits mangrove and paperbark swamps as well as rainforests around Australia's east and north coasts.

BEHAVIOUR: In the north of its range, large colonies of hundreds of thousands of Black Flying-foxes may form, although smaller camps are more common. Breed from Oct–Dec.

THREATS: Pythons, owls and crocodiles.

DIET: Fruit, flowers of gums, paperbarks, turpentines

LENGTH: HB 24–26 cm; Forearm 15–18.2 cm

WEIGHT: 500–700 g

STATUS: Vulnerable (NSW); Secure elsewhere

Spectacled Flying-fox *Pteropus conspicillatus*

Spectacled Flying-foxes are named for the rufous-tinged rings around their eyes. They are important seed dispersal animals for rainforest trees and are known to help spread the seeds of about 26 species.

BEHAVIOUR: Camps comprise thousands of individuals in mangroves and rainforests, but they fly out in pairs to feed at dusk. They have one young from Oct–Dec.

THREATS: Paralysis ticks, land clearing, electric/barbed wire fences and shooting.

DIET: Flowers and rainforest fruit

LENGTH: HB 22–24 cm; Forearm 15.5–18 cm

WEIGHT: 500–850 g

STATUS: Vulnerable (Cmwth)

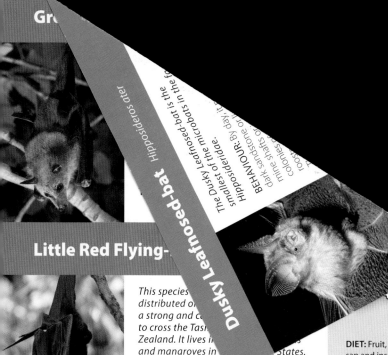

Gr...

Dusky Leafnosed-bat *Hippposideros ater*

The Dusky Leafnosed-bat is the ...
smallest of the microbats in the f...
Hipposideridae.

BEHAVIOUR: By day it ...
dark sandstone o...
mine shafts ...
colonies ...
roost...

Little Red Flying-...

This species ...
distributed o...
a strong and c...
to cross the Tas...
Zealand. It lives i...
and mangroves in ... States.

BEHAVIOUR: This is a nomadic species
that sometimes forms camps of up to a
million bats. At dusk they spiral up from the
canopy and fly out to feed.

THREATS: Raptors, reptiles and fishes.

DIET: Fruit, bark, leaves,
sap and insects

LENGTH:
HB 19.5–23.5 cm;
Forearm 12.5–15.6 cm

WEIGHT: 310–604 g

STATUS: Secure

Eastern Tube-nosed Bat *Nyctimene robinsoni*

The Eastern Tube-nosed Bat is a smaller
megabat relative of the flying-foxes. Its
yellow-spotted wings and ears, coupled
with its protruding "tube-like" nose,
make this species easy to identify. It
is a frequent visitor to orchards and
backyard fruit trees.

BEHAVIOUR: Solitary, but may gather in
groups of five. Usually feeds while hanging
upside down. Males make a bleating call.

THREATS: Habitat destruction.

DIET: Fruit, banksia
blossoms

LENGTH: HB 10–11 cm;
Forearm 6–7 cm;
T 2–2.5 cm

WEIGHT: 30–50 g

STATUS: Vulnerable
(NSW); Secure
elsewhere

...amily

...prefers to roost in ...mestone caves, in old ...n tree hollows, usually in ...r around 40 individuals. Often ...s are shared with other bat species. ...hey fly slowly and close to the ground, hovering when hunting insects.

THREATS: Ghost Bats and land clearing.

DIET: Moths and other insects
LENGTH: HB 4.5 cm; Forearm 3.7–4.3 cm; T 2.3–2.8 cm
WEIGHT: 4.5–10 g
STATUS: Secure

Ghost Bat *Macroderma gigas*

This is Australia's largest microbat and is largely carnivorous, feeding on insects, reptiles, amphibians, birds and small mammals. It has very good eyesight but still uses echolocation to find food.

BEHAVIOUR: Roosts by day in caves, crevices and disused mine shafts in northern Australia. Breeding occurs from Sept–Nov, with a single offspring produced every time.

THREATS: Snakes, owls and land clearing.

DIET: Reptiles, frogs, birds, mammals, insects
LENGTH: HB 10–13 cm; Forearm 10.2–11.2 cm
WEIGHT: 140–165 g
STATUS: Vulnerable (Qld); Endangered (SA); Near Threatened (NT)

Eastern Freetail-bat *Mormopterus norfolkensis*

Freetail-bats have a long tail that extends behind them further up the uropatagium (the membrane between the back legs) and is therefore known as a "free" tail. In spite of its scientific name, it is not found on Norfolk Island.

BEHAVIOUR: Sexes are probably segregated for at least part of the year, but little else is known about their breeding. They are mostly arboreal and roost in the trees.

THREATS: Probably snakes and owls.

DIET: Insects
LENGTH: HB 5–5.5 cm; T 3.5–4.5 cm Forearm 3.6–4 cm
WEIGHT: 7–10 g
STATUS: Vulnerable (NSW); Secure (Qld)

White-striped Freetail-bat *Tadarida australis*

This is the largest of Australia's freetail-bats and is somewhat grotesque, with large, misshapen ears. The White-striped Freetail-bat forages for insects and moths above the canopy of trees.

BEHAVIOUR: This bat species often also forages on the ground and is able to take off directly from the ground. They roost in tree hollows in small groups of up to ten, only forming large camps when breeding.

THREATS: Snakes, owls and land clearing.

DIET: Insects and moths
LENGTH: HB 8.5–10 cm; Forearm 5.7–6.3 cm; T 4–5 cm
WEIGHT: 25–40 g
STATUS: Near Threatened (IUCN Red List)

Eastern False Pipistrelle *Falsistrellus tasmaniensis*

Pipistrelles are microbats in the family Vespertilionid, one of the most successful of all bat families. They have large wings and probably forage widely.

BEHAVIOUR: Eastern False Pipstrelles may roost in the stem holes of eucalypts and are thought to roost in separate colonies for each sex, at least for some part of the year. They hibernate in winter.

THREATS: Pesticides and loss/clearing of roost trees.

DIET: Insects
LENGTH: HB 5.5–7 cm; Forearm 5–5 cm; T 4–5 cm
WEIGHT: 14–26 g
STATUS: Vulnerable (NSW); Rare (SA); Secure elsewhere

Northern Long-eared Bat
Nyctophilus arnhemensis

This species was first discovered in 1895 but was incorrectly identified — a mistake that was recognised only when a specimen was found at Rocky Bay, NT, in 1948.

BEHAVIOUR: Prefers habitat with annual rainfall of 500 mm and is commonly seen in mangrove forests. Has a fluttering, slow flying style with high manoeuvrability. Roosts in Cajeput trees and under awnings and roofs. Gives birth to twins.

THREATS: Clearing of roost trees.

DIET: Insects
LENGTH: HB 4.3–5.2 cm; Forearm 3.6–4 cm; T 3.5–4.3 cm
WEIGHT: 6–8 g
STATUS: Secure in limited range

Gould's Long-eared Bat *Nyctophilus gouldi*

This microbat species changes roosts frequently and may curl up under peeling bark, in tree hollows or in artificial nesting boxes. It is thought that males and females may roost in separate colonies.

BEHAVIOUR: Usually ambushes its insect prey by waiting in low foliage, then dropping down to devour insects that land below. Fat is stored in autumn for winter hibernation.

THREATS: Clearing of roost sites.

DIET: Insects
LENGTH:
HB 5.5–6.5 cm;
Forearm 3.4–4.8 cm;
T 4.5–5.5 cm
WEIGHT: 9–13 g
STATUS: Endangered (SA); Secure elsewhere

Eastern Horseshoe-bat *Rhinolophus megaphyllus*

Horseshoe-bats are named after their wrinkled U-shaped noseleafs. This species has been known to fly into houses seeking moths and insects, and sometimes roosts under eaves on verandahs.

BEHAVIOUR: Also known to roost in caves, abandoned bunkers, boulder piles and disused mine shafts. It seldom forms large camps of more than 2000 bats. Flies close to the canopy.

THREATS: Damage to roost sites.

DIET: Insects (largely caught in flight), spiders
LENGTH: HB 4.2–5.8 cm; Forearm 4.4–5.1 cm; T 3.8–4.3 cm
WEIGHT: 7–14 g
STATUS: Threatened (Vic); Secure elsewhere

Little Broad-nosed Bat *Scotorepens greyii*

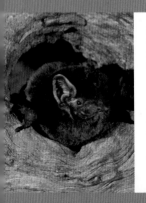

Habitats are hot and arid across most of this species' range, so it probably requires regular access to water, and flies out to drink at early evening.

BEHAVIOUR: Roosts mainly in tree hollows but has also been known to roost in abandoned buildings. Feeding begins at dusk on open woodlands and near creeks and waterways. Gives birth to twins (births likely to occur in Dec).

THREATS: Clearing of roost/feed sites.

DIET: Insects
LENGTH: HB 4.5–5.5 cm; Forearm 2.8–3.4 cm; T 2.5–4.0 cm
WEIGHT: 8–12 g
STATUS: Secure

Eastern Broad-nosed Bat *Scotorepens orion*

Tall, wet eucalypt forest is the preferred habitat for this species, which is confined to regions east of the Great Dividing Range.

BEHAVIOUR: It is known to roost in tree hollows, Manna Gums, and occasionally under overhanging roofs. More research is needed to determine diet and reproductive behaviour, but females have a single offspring in late spring/early summer.

THREATS: Interference with roosts.

DIET: Diet is little known, but probably insects

LENGTH: HB 4.3–5.4 cm; Forearm 32.5–37.5 cm; T 2.9–3.8 cm

WEIGHT: 7–15 g

STATUS: Secure

Common Blossom-bat *Syconycteris australis*

In spite of their diminutive size, blossom-bats are megabats and are mainly nectarivores, gathering nectar and pollen with their long, bristly tongues.

BEHAVIOUR: Common Blossom-bats are solitary and prefer to roost alone, hanging suspended from dense vegetation. Flight is usually around 3–5 m above the ground. One offspring is born from Oct–Nov.

THREATS: Habitat clearing.

DIET: Nectar and pollen

LENGTH: HB 4–6 cm; Forearm 3.8–4.5 cm

WEIGHT: 16–26 g

STATUS: Vulnerable (NSW); Secure elsewhere

Common Sheathtail-bat *Taphozous georgianus*

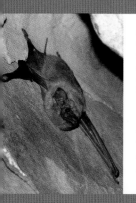

Sheathtail-bats are distinguished by a long tail and uropatagium skin flap between the tail and the back legs. Rather than dangle suspended from their roosts, these bats cling to the wall with the clawed toe at the end of the wing.

BEHAVIOUR: Common Sheathtail-bats roosts in cave overhangs or wedge themselves into crevices in the rocks. They are nocturnal. Most give birth to one offspring (Dec).

THREATS: Mining and land clearing.

DIET: Beetles and other insects

LENGTH: HB 7.5–8.9 cm; Forearm 6.6–7.4 cm; T 2.1–3.2 cm

WEIGHT: 19–51 g

STATUS: Secure

Rats & Mice

Australia has 64 native rodent species that inhabit a range of environments — some, like the Water-rat, are even semi-aquatic. All rodents are characterised by their long, chisel-like incisors. These four teeth continue to grow over the rodent's life and must be kept at a reasonable length by gnawing. Many species in the family Muridae are known as "old endemics" — early rodents that are unique to this continent. "New endemics" arrived on these shores only within the last few million years and are related to European rodents in the subfamily Murinae.

Water-rat *Hydromys chrysogaster*

Dense, waterproof fur helps the amphibious Water-rat stay warm and dry. Water-rats hunt invertebrates, fishes, frogs and birds both on land and underwater. When not hunting, they rest on the shore in hollow logs or burrows.

BEHAVIOUR: Water-rats are active by day and night and able to breed year round, giving birth to three or four offspring up to five times a year.

THREATS: Pollution of waterways.

DIET: Crustaceans, aquatic insects, fishes, frogs, small mammals and waterbirds

LENGTH: HB 23.1–37 cm; T 22.7–32.5 cm

WEIGHT: 340–1275 g

STATUS: Secure

Greater Stick-nest Rat *Leporillus conditor*

Unfortunately, this nest-building rodent has become locally extinct on the mainland and now survives only on Franklin Island, SA. It builds an elaborate 1 m high by 1.5 m wide nest that it shares with up to twenty individuals.

BEHAVIOUR: The Greater Stick-nest Rat is strictly herbivorous and nocturnal. It is also highly gregarious. Breeding is year round, but peaks from autumn–winter with 1–3 offspring in a litter.

THREATS: Cats, foxes, raptors and owls.

DIET: Leaves and fruit of native species

LENGTH: HB 17–26 cm; Tail 14.5–18 cm

WEIGHT: 180–450 g

STATUS: Endangered (IUCN Red List); Vulnerable (Cmwth)

Grassland Melomys *Melomys burtoni*

The Grassland Melomys has wide hindfeet and a partly prehensile tail, making it a competent climber; however, it is mostly ground-dwelling and is particularly fond of canefields.

BEHAVIOUR: This solitary species constructs round nests of shredded plants up to a metre above ground, sometimes in hollow logs or under bark in rainforest environments.

THREATS: Cats, foxes, Dingoes and owls.

DIET: Plant stems, seeds, fruit and insects
LENGTH: HB 9–16 cm; T 10–17.5 cm
WEIGHT: 26–124 g
STATUS: Secure

Cape York Melomys *Melomys capensis*

A long, sparsely furred prehensile tail suits this melomys' partly arboreal life. It is larger than its grassland relative and dwells in rainforests, where its population swells when fruit is in season.

BEHAVIOUR: Nests during the day in leaf-lined tree hollows and forages by night in leaf litter or in the trees. Females are mature at just 80 days and give birth to two young per litter.

THREATS: White-tailed Rats and cats.

DIET: Fruit, leaves, shoots and seeds
LENGTH:
HB 11.9–16.2 cm; T 12.9–17.2 cm
WEIGHT: 45–116 g
STATUS: Secure

Golden-backed Tree-rat *Mesembriomys macrurus*

These rodents occupy a home range of up to 600 m, which is shared by two breeding adults and some juveniles (probably their offspring). Their range has decreased since they were first recorded in 1875.

BEHAVIOUR: Golden-backed Tree-rats are nocturnal and arboreal, but are known to forage on the beach and in rainforest leaf litter. Breeds all year.

THREATS: Cats, owls, raptors, foxes and Dingoes.

DIET: Flowers, fruit, termites, leaves, grass
LENGTH:
HB 18.8–24.5 cm; T 29.1–36 cm
WEIGHT: 207–330 g
STATUS: Vulnerable (Cmwth); Endangered (NT)

Spinifex Hopping-mouse *Notomys alexis*

The tiny, large-eared Spinifex Hopping-mouse is an aridland specialist. It excavates 1 m deep burrows (with many entrances as escape routes) to avoid the desert heat. After rain, populations flourish.

BEHAVIOUR: Spinifex Hopping-mice are nocturnal, terrestrial and mostly quadrupedal, but swiftly hop away on the back legs if threatened. Breeding peaks in spring.

THREATS: Birds of prey and feral cats.

DIET: Insects and other invertebrates, seeds, leaves and roots

LENGTH: HB 9.5–11.2 cm; T 13.1–15 cm

WEIGHT: 27–45 g

STATUS: Secure

Dusky Hopping-mouse *Notomys fuscus*

Explorer Charles Sturt was referring to this species when he wrote of Indigenous hunters carrying "bags full of jerboas". Today, this pretty little rodent is one of the least-seen mammals and is considered vulnerable.

BEHAVIOUR: Another arid-adapted rodent, it burrows into sand dunes and shares a nest of chewed-up grass with five others.

THREATS: Dingoes, cats and raptors.

DIET: Seeds, plants and some insects

LENGTH: HB 8–11.5 cm; T 11.5–15.5 cm

WEIGHT: 30–50 g

STATUS: Vulnerable (Cmwth); Endangered (NT, Qld & NSW)

Prehensile-tailed Rat *Pogonomys mollipilosus*

The long, slender tail of this rat is its most splendid feature and is able to suspend the rat's entire body weight. It was first discovered in 1974 in a cat's jaws!

BEHAVIOUR: Nocturnal and partly arboreal, they sleep by day in a burrow in the leaf litter. Each burrow has a hidden escape tunnel to help them avoid predation. They are mostly solitary but sometimes feed in small groups of up to three.

THREATS: Pythons, quolls and owls.

DIET: Leaves and fruit

LENGTH: HB 12–16.5 cm; T 16–20.8 cm

WEIGHT: 42–83 g

STATUS: Secure

Plains Rat *Pseudomys australis*

In the harsh, arid environments in which this rodent lives, water is frequently unavailable; instead, Plains Rats get all their liquid nourishment from their diet of seeds, stems and insects.

BEHAVIOUR: Plains Rats are nocturnal, terrestrial and sociable (with up to 20 rats sharing a burrow system). Populations flourish after rain, and young leave the nest at just four weeks.

THREATS: Dingoes, foxes and owls.

DIET: Stems, leaves, seeds and insects

LENGTH: HB 10–14 cm; T 8–12 cm

WEIGHT: 50–80 g

STATUS: Vulnerable (Cmwth); Endangered (Qld & NT); Extinct (NSW)

Delicate Mouse *Pseudomys delicatulus*

Naturalist John Gould once wrote that this species was the tiniest, most attractive mouse species in Australia, similar in appearance to the English Harvest Mouse. However dainty it is, he was not correct in calling it the smallest; other species are just as tiny.

BEHAVIOUR: Terrestrial and nocturnal, spending the day in shallow burrows with one entrance. Irruptions occur after rain.

THREATS: Cats, owls, foxes and snakes.

DIET: Grasses, seeds and grains

LENGTH: HB 5.5–7.5 cm; T 5.5–8 cm

WEIGHT: 6–15 g

STATUS: Near Threatened (IUCN Red List)

Eastern Chestnut Mouse
Pseudomys gracilicaudatus

This small mouse shares similar habitat to the larger Swamp Rat, which may displace it in some areas. Most individuals seldom stray from their tiny home range of just 0.5 ha.

BEHAVIOUR: More crepuscular than most, but still mostly nocturnal. It uses runways in vegetation to travel from nests/burrows to feeding sites. Short gestation period and early maturity aid population growth.

THREATS: Competition and carnivores.

DIET: Plant stems, leaves, seeds, fungi and insects

LENGTH: HB 10.5–14.5 cm; T 8–12 cm

WEIGHT: 45–118 g

STATUS: Vulnerable (NSW); Secure elsewhere

Sandy Inland Mouse *Pseudomys hermannsburgensis*

This small native mouse looks rather like the common introduced House Mouse but is usually a paler sandy brown. It is also less smelly than the House Mouse and does not have a musky odour.

BEHAVIOUR: Nests by day in a 50 cm deep burrow that it sometimes shares with the Knob-tailed Gecko. Irruptions occur after rainfall, and breeding appears to be year round.

THREATS: Cats, owls and mouse traps.

DIET: Seeds, grass shoots, tubers, roots and invertebrates

LENGTH: HB 6.5–8.5 cm; T 7–9 cm

WEIGHT: 9–14.5 g

STATUS: Vulnerable (Qld); Secure elsewhere

New Holland Mouse *Pseudomys novaehollandiae*

After seemingly vanishing for more than 120 years, the New Holland Mouse was rediscovered in Sydney's Ku-ring-gai Chase National Park, NSW, in 1967.

BEHAVIOUR: Known to favour areas that have been burnt and regenerated where its diet is seasonally variable. It is a nocturnal burrower that lives in small groups. Populations peak in autumn.

THREATS: Cats, foxes and owls.

DIET: Seeds, flowers, fungi, insects and invertebrates

LENGTH: HB 6.5–8.8 cm; T 8.1–10.7 cm

WEIGHT: 12–26 g

STATUS: Threatened (Vic); Endangered (Tas)

Eastern Pebble-mound Mouse
Pseudomys patrius

This rare and vulnerable mouse was first recorded in 1900. Extraordinarily, it is able to use its mouth to carry 5 g pebbles to a "mound" it carefully arranges around the entrance to its burrow.

BEHAVIOUR: More research into this mouse's behaviour is needed. It is thought that the pebbles help accumulate dew and water in the mouse's arid habitat.

THREATS: Cats, owls and snakes.

DIET: Seeds, grasses and other plants, insects

LENGTH: HB c. 7 cm; T c. 7.5 cm

WEIGHT: 12 g

STATUS: Vulnerable (IUCN Red List)

Bush Rat *Rattus fuscipes*

The Bush Rat is a "new endemic" that is common in parts along the south-eastern coast but is rarely seen. Each autumn, almost all of the breeding adults die, leaving populations of juveniles that will mate in the spring.

BEHAVIOUR: All four Bush Rat subspecies are solitary and rest by day in tunnels beneath shrubby/ferny cover, hunting insects by night.

THREATS: Logging, fire, cats and owls.

DIET: Insects, fungi, fruit, seeds, stems of grasses

LENGTH:
HB 11.1–21.4 cm;
T 10.5–19.5 cm

WEIGHT: 40–225 g

STATUS: Secure throughout range

False Water-rat *Xeromys myoides*

Since it was first discovered in 1889, this species has been rarely collected and is little known. It is one of the only animals able to eat a type of toxic flatworm. It may cover up to 2 km a night while searching for prey.

BEHAVIOUR: Nocturnal and terrestrial, sharing a communal nest/burrow with eight others. Although strong swimmers, they are not aquatic like the "true" Water-rat.

THREATS: Mangrove destruction.

DIET: Crustaceans, flatworms, other mangrove invertebrates

LENGTH:
HB 8.7–11.9 cm;
T 7–9.1 cm

WEIGHT: 32–54 g

STATUS: Vulnerable (Cmwth & IUCN Red List)

Common Rock-rat *Zyzomys argurus*

Also sometimes known as the Thick-tailed Rat, the Common Rock-rat is a widely distributed inhabitant of rocky habitats in the tropical north. Its extremely long tail is susceptible to damage and often withers away to a stump when injured.

BEHAVIOUR: The Common Rock-rat is terrestrial and nocturnal, but clumps of chewed up seeds may betray its daytime hiding places in rocky crevices.

THREATS: Feral cats, owls and raptors.

DIET: Leaves, stems, seeds, insects and fungi

LENGTH:
HB 8.5–12.2 cm;
T up to 12.5 cm

WEIGHT: 26–55 g

STATUS: Secure

Dingo
Canis lupus dingo

Widely regarded as Australia's native wild dog, the Dingo (which shares the family Canidae with domestic dogs and the introduced Red Fox) is actually a relatively recent arrival to these shores. Dingoes can trace their lineage to the Indian Wolf (*Canis lupus pallipes*), and some believe they represent Australia's first deliberately introduced mammal. Whether Aboriginal or Asian people orchestrated their arrival on this continent around 3000 years ago is unknown. (Aborigines have enjoyed a close relationship with Dingoes, but strong natural instincts make them difficult to domesticate.) Animals in the family Canidae have non-retractable claws and long muzzles armed with sharp canine teeth.

Dingoes are the largest carnivorous mammals on the continent, with a fossil record that traces them back more than 3000 years. Despite being befriended by Aborigines, who used them for hunting, Dingoes have never been truly domesticated. Unless kept with domestic dogs, they do not bark and use howls and sharp "yaps" to communicate. Unfortunately, crossbreeding with feral domestic dogs has affected 80–100% of mainland Dingo packs. Purebred Dingoes on Fraser Island, Qld, now represent one of the last genetically unaltered populations.

FEATURES: Most are ginger to tan, although they may also be a darker red or even black. All have paler (usually white) lower paws (socks) and white on the tip of the tail. Many have black or white on the muzzle, and most have a white underbelly. The teeth and skull are larger than in domestic dogs.

DIET & HABITAT: Most Australian habitats suit these large mammals that are known to hunt by day or by night, but are mostly considered crepuscular. They are opportunistic eaters, feeding on small mammals such as rodents, possums and dasyurids; larger kangaroos, wombats and wallabies; feral mammals; livestock; insects and birds — even fruit and carrion in some instances.

BEHAVIOUR: Dingoes live, and sometimes hunt, in packs of up to twelve family members that share a territory of around 8000 ha. Howls are used to greet the pack, which is dominated by one breeding pair.

BREEDING: Pairs mate for life and have a litter of up to ten pups every year (born during late autumn or winter). Pups remain in a den and suckle for 3–4 months before beginning to hunt.

THREATS: Poison baits, crossbreeding with feral dogs, shooting and trapping.

DIET: Other mammals (hunting larger animals in packs), bird, reptiles, carrion and fruit

LENGTH: HB 86–122 cm; T 26–38 cm
WEIGHT: 9.6–24 kg
STATUS: Secure

Above: Dingoes in a wide range of colours occupy most mainland habitats, including tropical grasslands, high country, coastal heath, saltbush and aridlands.

Introduced Mammals

Before European occupation of Australia, the continent was home to just one large carnivore and no hard-hoofed animals. Over the past 200 years, 23 mammal species have been introduced — all of which have done considerable damage to habitats and their native residents.

Some were the product of farming; others, like the House Mouse, were stowaways that quickly became pests. Still others, such as rabbits, deer and the Red Fox, were introduced purely as sport for Europeans who favoured hunting. Introduced mammals increase competition for food, displace or prey upon native wildlife, and may also destroy natural environments — either through their habits (as in wallowing feral pigs and buffalo) or simply by their presence.

Hard-hoofed grazing stock (such as cows, sheep, goats and horses), coupled with over-grazing, have damaged natural grasslands and exacerbated the effects of soil erosion. For an ancient land with a fragile, often sparsely vegetated surface, this is a real problem. Compounding the issue, large tracts of land have been cleared of their natural vegetation so that crops and grasses could flourish, which has affected those species that are highly reliant on native flora.

Camels, although less hard-hoofed than stock, were brought to Australia to help explorers penetrate the arid outback. Once journeys were complete, many were set free and quickly became feral. Goats, donkeys and wild horses (brumbies) also rapidly established a niche in well-vegetated areas of the continent.

Introduced carnivores have had a devastating impact on native wildlife. Cats, foxes and feral dogs are ruthless predators of native birds, rodents, reptiles and small mammals. However detrimental, these animals do not rival the damage done by Australia's most common and most invasive introduced mammal — ourselves.

Top to bottom: Feral dogs crossbreed with the Dingo; Hoofed mammals increase soil erosion.
Opposite: Rabbits, goats, deer and donkeys compete with native grazing animals. Pigs and buffalo ruin native waterways. Cats and foxes prey on native fauna.

Glossary

ARBOREAL Living in trees.

CAECUM Part of the large intestine. Most herbivores have an enlarged caecum to assist with breaking down cellulose contained in plants.

CHROMOSOME A thread of genes and DNA found in the nucleus of a cell. Different organisms have different numbers of chromosomes.

CLOACA Posterior chamber of the gut in monotremes and marsupials where the urinary tract and female reproductive system end.

CREPUSCULAR Active at dawn and dusk.

DENTITION Relating to the teeth.

DICOTYLEDONOUS (PLANT) Group of flowering plants where the seed typically features two embryonic leaves.

DIURNAL Active during the day.

DREY A nest used by possums, etc.

EMBRYO An animal in developmental stage between conception and birth.

EMBRYONIC DIAPAUSE State of arrested development in a viable embryo, which may be carried in the uterus for some months.

FERAL Having reverted to a wild state.

FORB A special type of flowering plant with a non-woody stem. Not in the general category of a grass, shrub or tree.

GESTATION Time between conception and birth.

GREGARIOUS Social, living in groups.

HEATHLAND Vegetation dominated by hard-leaved, small shrubs (usually less than 2 m high) growing in poor, sandy soils.

HERBIVORE Animal that eats plants.

HOME RANGE Area an animal traverses during its normal daily activities.

HYBRID The offspring of two different species.

IUCN RED LIST A list describing the conservation status of threatened species published by the International Union for the Conservation of Nature and Natural Resources.

MARSUPIUM Pouch, a distinguishing feature of most female marsupials.

MEGAFAUNA Large mammal species that survived in Australia during the Pleistocene Epoch.

NOCTURNAL Active during the night.

OESTROUS CYCLE A period of sexual receptivity in females, caused by reproductive hormones that stimulate the release of an ovum (egg) ready to be fertilised by the male.

PATAGIUM In a gliding mammal, the membrane that stretches between forelimbs and hindlimbs.

PENTAPEDAL (GAIT) Five-limbed movement.

PREHENSILE Able to grip.

QUADRUPEDAL (GAIT) Four-limbed movement.

SCLEROPHYLL (FOREST) Forest dominated by sclerophyllous (hard-leaved) trees, especially eucalypts.

SUCCULENT A fleshy or juicy plant.

SUPERNUMERARY More than the usual number of body parts.

SYNDACTYLUS Condition where two or more digits are fused together.

TAXONOMY The scientific practice of classifying life.

UNDERSTOREY The shrubs, saplings and plants that grow under the forest canopy.

VOLPLANE To glide through the air.

WOODLAND Area sparsely covered by trees.

Index

Links & Further Reading

Books

Currey, K. *Fact File: Mammals*, Steve Parish Publishing, Brisbane, 2006

Curtis, L. K, *Green Guide; Kangaroos & Wallabies of Australia*, New Holland, Sydney, 2006

Egerton, L. (Ed) *Encylopedia of Australia Wildlife*, Reader's Digest, Sydney, 2005

Grigg, G. Jarman, P & Hume, I (Eds.) *Kangaroos, Wallabies and Rat-kangaroos*, 3 vols, Surrey, Beatty and Sons, Sydney, 1989

Jones, C. & Parish, S. *Field Guide to Australian Mammals*, Steve Parish Publishing, Brisbane, 2004

Lindsey, T. *Green Guide: Mammals of Australia*, New Holland, Sydney, 1998

Menkhorst, P. & Knight, F. *Field Guide to the Mammals of Australia*, Oxford University Press, Melbourne, 2001

Strahan, Ronald (Ed.) *The Mammals of Australia*, Reed New Holland, Sydney, 2002

Watts, D. *Kangaroos & Wallabies of Australia*, New Holland, Sydney, 1999

Websites

Action Plan for Australian Marsupials and Monotremes **www.environment.gov. au/biodiversity/threatened/publications/ action/marsupials/**

Australian Government: Department of the Environment and Water Resources **www. environment.gov.au/biodiversity/trade-use/wild-harvest/kangaroo/**

Australian Museum **www.amonline.net. au/mammals/resources/links.htm**

IUCN Red List of Threatened Species **www. iucnredlist.org/**

Marsupial Society of Australia **www. marsupialsociety.org/**

Australiasian Bat Society **http://ausbats.org.au**

Australian Mammal Society **www. australianmammals.org.au**

CSIRO Sustainable Ecosystems **www.cse. csiro.au**

Published by Steve Parish Publishing Pty Ltd
PO Box 1058, Archerfield, Qld 4108 Australia

www.steveparish.com.au

© Steve Parish Publishing

ISBN: 978174193325 3

First published 2008

Principal photography: Steve Parish

Additional photography: Allan Fox: p. 13 (3rd
from top & bottom); Martin Harvey/ANTPhoto.
com: p. 82 (top); Bruce Thomson/ANTPhoto:
p. 95 (top); Dave Watts/ANTPhoto.com: p. 19
(bottom right); Pavel German/Auscape: pp.
49 (top left) & 68; Mike Gillam/Auscape: p.
41; Suzanne Long/Auscape: p. 49 (bottom
left); Michael Cermak: pp. 51 (bottom) & 100
(bottom); Les Hall: pp. 93 (bottom), 94 (top), 95
(centre & bottom) & 97 (centre); Jiri Lochman/
Lochman Transparencies: pp. 28 (bottom), 47
(top), 63, 72 (bottom) & 79 (bottom); Marie
Lochman/Lochman Transparencies: p. 74
(bottom); Dave Watts/Lochman Transparencies:
pp. 47 (centre) & 73 (bottom); M & I Morcombe:
pp. 24 (bottom), 26 (top), 30, 33–34, 40 (top),
51 (top), 53 & 65 (top left); Ian Morris: pp. 14
(left), 25 (centre), 26 (centre), 27 (top), 28 (top),
29 (bottom), 38 (centre), 39 (top & centre), 50
(bottom), 64, 79 (centre), 80 (top), 92 (top), 97
(bottom), 99, 103 (bottom) & 105 (top left);
Bruce Cowell/Queensland Museum: pp. 6
(bottom), 26 (bottom), 58 & 102 (bottom); Jeff
Wright/Queensland Museum: pp. 101 (centre) &
102 (top); Queensland Museum: p. 21 (bottom
left), 29 (top & centre), 49 (top right), 50 (top),
90 (bottom), 98 (top), 100 (centre), 101 (bottom),
102 (centre) & 103 (top & centre)

Front cover image: Common Wombat

Title page image: Sugar Glider. Inset, top to
bottom: Platypus; Koala.

Text: Karin Cox, SPP
Editorial: Les Savage; Ted Lewis &
Michele Perry, SPP
Design: Leanne Nobilio, SPP
Production: Tina Brewster, SPP

Prepress by Colour Chiefs Digital Imaging,
Brisbane, Australia
Printed in Singapore by Imago

**Produced in Australia at the Steve Parish
Publishing Studios**